BURNED

Wounded Women Series

Betrayed

Broken

Burned

Introvert, She Wrote

Quiet & Badass

Gemini Moon Press

Lunar Wisdom

Lunar Magic (coming 2024)

BURNED

Brave and Inspiring Stories From
Women Who Have Overcome Their
Fears To Speak Their Truth And Share
Their Wisdom

Curated by Jenny Alberti
and Tracey Brown

Women Writing Intentionally Collective

Copyright © 2024 by Women Writing Intentionally Collective LLC

All rights reserved. No portion of this book may be reproduced in any form without written permission from the publisher or author, except as permitted by U.S. copyright law.

This publication is sold with the understanding that neither the author nor the publisher is engaged in rendering legal, investment, accounting, or other professional services. While the publisher and authors have used their best efforts in preparing this book, they make no representations or warranties with respect to the accuracy or completeness of the contents of this book and specifically disclaim any implied warranties of merchantability or fitness for a particular purpose. The advice and strategies contained herein may not be suitable for your situation. You should consult with a professional when appropriate. Neither the publisher nor the authors shall be liable for any loss of profit or any other commercial damages, including but not limited to special, incidental, consequential, personal, or other damages.

Book Cover by Camilla Fellas Arnold

E-book ISBN: 978-1-959509-05-9
Paperback ISBN: 978-1-959509-07-3

Disclaimer and Content Warning

The publisher takes no legal responsibility for the details inside the stories of this book. The words and opinions are the authors' own, and the memories they describe are their lived experiences. Some of the stories contained within may be disturbing for some readers, as they explore themes related to alcohol consumption, domestic abuse and/or sexual trauma, eating disorders, suicide attempts, and mental health concerns. Readers are advised to seek professional or medical assistance as necessary.

CONTENTS

Introduction		1
1.	Burning With Words Amanda Norr	5
2.	That 'Annoying' Girl Who Dared to Speak Kaitlyn Signorelli	8
3.	In Fire Corinne Schwers	14
4.	Coded For Silence, Destined to Speak: One Woman's Search for Her True Voice Carolyn Parker	18
5.	Flames of Healing Christine Frey	25
6.	The Beautiful Bridge Teri Katzenberger	33

7.	Breaking The Chains: Unleashing My Voice To Reclaim My Power Laura Rinnankoski	51
8.	Phoenix Rising Tara Haislip	57
9.	There's More To Life Than Just Fish Jennifer Arwen Templeton	63
10.	The Quiet Revolution: Finding My Own Voice Jamila Ekkel	71
11.	This Witch Won't Burn Tracey Brown	82
12.	Unraveling The Witch Wound Stephanie Moyer	103
13.	Start The Conversation Linsey Joy	109
14.	Speak Your Truth Jenny Alberti	116
15.	Reclaiming The Witch Kelli Femrite	129
	Meet The Authors	143

INTRODUCTION

When we first came up with the *Wounded Women Series* trilogy concept, *Burned* was meant to be the second title in the series after *Betrayed*. There was something about the "betrayed, burned, and broken" that just rolled off the tongue and felt right when it came to the flow of the book titles and their messages.

A short time later, we received a nudge from the Universe that *Broken* and *Burned* needed to swap places and, with the fresh-faced naivety and optimism that came with the start of our journey on the 'Path of the Wounded Women,' we accepted the change without question. We have since come to understand that *Burned* needed more time before being created and released into the world. That there were women we needed to meet and experiences that needed to unfold. In rolling with the flow of the Universe, and not forcing things to happen according to an arbitrary schedule we'd decided upon, we've allowed ourselves to embrace the plan the Universe has, and revel in the magic that transpired along the way. In flipping the order of publication of *Broken* and *Burned*, we are confident that everything has ultimately worked out exactly as it was supposed to.

But it wasn't only the order in which *Burned* was released that changed. The original subtitle was, *Women Who Have Overcome The Witch Wound To Speak Their Truth And Share Their Wisdom Without Fear*, but Jenny proposed that, in order to make the title more attractive for the women we wanted to call in as potential authors, we should drop the word 'witch' from the title altogether.

Hello, manifestation of the Witch Wound!

The collective trauma that we, as women, carry from generations of persecution, torture, and outright, brutal murder is embedded so deeply deep in our psyche—and epigenetic memory—that even though we may be aware of its existence, there are still so many layers to pull back, reveal, and explore, and there is much work still to be done to heal and release it.

Yes, let us be the first to admit that even though we were well aware of the symptoms of the Witch Wound, at the beginning of our journey on the 'Path of the Wounded Women,' we still fell victim to the belief that we needed to make the book more socially acceptable if we wanted to succeed. Since the success of our series hinged on women wanting to participate as authors, we felt that age-old need to conform to survive, and it was a case of 'change the title of the book to be more socially acceptable—OR ELSE.' Proof, even for us, that the Witch Wound is alive and well!

Our goal for this book was to shine a light and raise awareness of the Witch and Healer Wounds. We wanted to provide a safe space for our authors to share their own experiences in dealing with and working to heal these wounds so that, together, we could lay foundations for the healing of the collective. We believe that when one woman does work to heal her wound, it contributes to the healing of all past, present, and future generations.

INTRODUCTION

As far back as September 2022, we talked about how we knew that walking the 'Path of the Wounded Women' was going to be transformative for each of us and yet, ironically, we had no idea of the depth of the unexpected revelations, awakenings, and immense personal growth we would witness both within ourselves and for each of our authors during the creation of this series, and the culmination of *Burned* itself.

The *Wounded Women Series* has been a living, breathing extension of us. It's been a deeply personal and integral part of our lives, embodying our thoughts, feelings, experiences, and values to such an extent that it feels like a part of our very existence. It has grown and evolved alongside us while we each grew and evolved alongside it.

To those of you who have walked with us and witnessed the journey unfold throughout *Betrayed*, *Broken*, and *Burned*, we thank you for sharing in the 'Path of the Wounded Women,' and we hope that you have found, recognised, healed, and released elements of your own wounds along the way.

If *Burned* is your introduction to the *Wounded Women Series*, we hope that it will inspire you to dive deeper and reexamine your past experiences, beliefs, and patterns so you can shift, evolve, heal, and step into your full power, unapologetically.

The world needs your magic.

With all our love,
Jenny Alberti & Tracey Brown
Sacramento, California & Torino, Italy
January 2024

I
BURNING WITH WORDS
Amanda Norr

We are still being burned.
I watched them burn her.
Not with fire, but with words.
An attempt to ruin her reputation.
They had no proof.
Used it against her anyway.
They lied and maligned.
While she begged for her life.
Her crime was helping the helpless.
Her crime was calling out harm.
Her crime was helping me.
I watched, fearing I was next.
They didn't want me.
They wanted her silence.
She would not be silent.
They didn't want me!

I chose then, to walk away.
I will no longer sit down.
I will not play their games.
I found a way to walk free.
We will take their fire.
We will burn their structure down.
We know they see it coming.
We will rise from their ashes.

I AM A LIVING, breathing woman, feeling myself torn into fragments and barely being held together. I am curious to know: What is holding me together? Why am I in fragments? It's the Witch Wound. I am not able to be my whole self all the time for the fear of speaking up.

Having grown and changed so much in the last several years, I have had to unlearn lifelong beliefs. To learn to embrace others' humanity as I learn to love my own.

In my desire to understand my pain and fear, I have studied the history of brave women who have spoken out. The right to vote has always been important to me. A few years ago, I began to hear stories of the brave suffragettes being beaten, jailed, and tortured. There are still many places around the world today where women and girls are punished for trying to get an education.

And a bit closer to home, there are women I know who are speaking out against church leaders for enabling abuse and teachings that lead to suicide for some, and extreme mental harm for others. It is a cautionary tale of tragedy. In my lifetime I have seen the attempt at silencing the successes of women in order to discredit and scare them. To discredit and scare us all.

Although I have been able to step out of my cage and share parts of my story in different places, I continue to feel afraid to do it all in one place. I know I am meant to break down barriers and I would like to do more than simply survive these experiences.

There are moments when I am terrified to let my whole self be seen. I have many interests and passions, and my personal ethics and values can be at odds with others' religious beliefs and politics, even when other core values align. I have been accused of, and judged for, things I have never said or would never have thought.

The answers have yet to appear, nor a map to take with me on this journey through the shadows of grief and fear. To learn when and where to speak and bring all my fragments together and whole into the light.

I do know that as we each work through our own obstacles, and reach out and seek each other, we will be able to stand together with our heads high and voices strong, leading a forward charge for those within power to see the reason to help us.

We will burn down their structures, those that have kept us in fear, with their own fires. In doing so, we show our daughters and granddaughters that they, too, have the power to join us and be fierce, and we honor our mothers' and grandmothers' pain and sacrifice. Together, we are rising.

2

THAT 'ANNOYING' GIRL WHO DARED TO SPEAK

Kaitlyn Signorelli

Too loud. Too quiet. Too sensitive. Too talkative. Too much. Lazy. Ditzy. Impulsive. Annoying. You're smart, but you do stupid things. Try harder. Stop being so dramatic. You're overreacting.

These are some of the phrases I grew up hearing about myself. The resounding message: I was never 'enough.' I was always doing something wrong, no matter how hard I tried.

It took decades to realize I wasn't *obligated to change myself* when people said those things to me; it didn't make me *less valuable*. Those judgments were projections of their insecurities and limiting beliefs. They had little (if anything) to do with *me*.

But before I knew this, I constantly felt that I was doing something 'wrong' to be perceived in those ways. As a result, I would edit my behavior and censor my words based on who I was around—performing the part of who I thought was most palatable for whatever environment

I was in. I thought I could avoid criticism and—maybe—avoid everyone realizing that I wasn't good enough.

It was *exhausting* to suppress my voice, my opinions, and my true self. In the moments I couldn't hold my personality back any longer, it came out messy and immature (duh, because I hadn't been nurturing and strengthening it). I held on to so much *shame* from those moments of 'weakness!'

There are many stories I could share but one stands out from the rest—the experience that shaped my entire life. One of my most painful memories that, now, I revere.

My first year in middle school, aged eleven, was traumatic. Bullying resulted in the abrupt loss of my physical and psychological safety. The situation eventually calmed down, and I began to relax.

Then I had a dream where I was rejected by my friends. My heart raced. Tears were in my eyes. I was unsettled. I was upset. But at least it was only a dream.

The next day, my friends and I were sitting at the lunch table when another girl abruptly cut me off from speaking. She berated me in front of everyone, "You're annoying. You talk too much. No one cares what you have to say." This came out of nowhere. She and I had never had issues before—in fact, she was new to the school and I knew what it had felt like for me to be the 'new girl' that year, so I had been kind to her and wanted to make sure she had a friend.

My mind received her words like this: *Nothing you have ever said, nothing that you will ever say, will matter to anyone—so shut up and stay quiet, because you are too annoying to inflict your talking onto anyone.*

My soul fractured that day. I was devastated! *I blamed myself for it happening*. I must actually be that annoying or it wouldn't have happened—and maybe I was the cause of everything that happened to me that year.

I tried to keep going as best I could. And, just when I thought I had made the necessary adjustments to fit in, it happened again. Same girl. Same words—with an added, "I told you, you weren't welcome here. Why are you back? Didn't you understand the first time? No one wants you here."

Clearly, I hadn't suppressed my annoyingness enough; I would have to try harder if I didn't want to keep being a target. *Her words* become *my inner voice*.

For the next decade, I tried to find a balance between being myself—but 'not too much' because then I'd be rejected, again. I had an inner world (the me I needed to protect, but who also desperately wanted to be seen and accepted), and a fragmented outer life (the chameleon, always changing to avoid predators who would swoop in to remind me I wasn't enough).

My depression became consuming. Anxiety replayed all my mistakes as I tried to sleep. And food became an enemy that I could control. If I couldn't fix my brain or personality, at least I could have an 'approved' body.

Yet my soul *craved* to speak. I *loved* to be on stage but I was 'annoying,' and no one wanted to hear *my words*. So I danced, sang, and performed in plays. I'd feel nervous about presenting in class, but I still enjoyed it. It was safe—no one could get mad at me for speaking. I won awards on the debate team for impromptu speaking where I practiced the technical skills of speaking: pace, tone, inflection, captivating attention.

But still, my inside-self felt *completely invisible* and resoundingly *unworthy*. So I kept seeking ways to become 'worthy enough' that my words would have their importance restored.

Eventually, I realized what I believed about my self-worth and how hard I was on myself had become a true matter of life or death. I discovered there were many layers and levels to healing this wound. It was not just one change or one insight that healed everything—it was a process.

As I reclaimed my worth, it felt *messy and chaotic!* I felt so much *anger*. I felt vulnerable and uncomfortable. But I couldn't go back to hiding—it had been killing me. I was determined to embody self-assurance and learn how to give myself the approval I had been so desperate to receive from everyone else.

Courageously, but not without fear, I started to create opportunities for myself to speak *my words*. It surprised me when people told me how much they enjoyed the experience, suggested that I should write a book, and even shared how I inspired them. Even with all this feedback, I still thought, *But if they get to know me, they'll find out how annoying I am.* However, I was also celebrating that inner voice becoming quieter.

Then all in a week after I became pregnant, I left a failing relationship, paused my graduate studies, and moved back in with my parents on the other side of the country—with no job, no health insurance, and no money. It looked like a truly rock bottom moment, yet instead of feeling helpless, I navigated it with utter determination to continue rebuilding my self-worth.

Part of that process was hiring my doula, Naomi, an advocate who knew my wishes and would help me speak if I wasn't being heard. I embodied the truth that I am worthy of having someone help *my voice* to be heard. Through this experience, I gained a deeper understanding of how to stand in my authority during challenges, taking part in creating outcomes instead of giving away my power. Exactly the behavior I wanted to model for my child!

Years later, I'd pull from my tarot cards and often receive the card for grief. I knew I'd healed much from middle school, but it still held sadness. One day, I pulled the card and decided to sit with the sadness—to give it space to exist with no expectations. I lit a candle, closed my eyes, and allowed my mind to wander.

The mermaid from my card invited me beneath her waters. We surfaced in my memory of that lunchtime. I wasn't expecting anything different than the numerous times I had revisited that moment, but this quickly took a turn.

The cafeteria became empty; only tables, chairs, myself, and my guide remained. The room was then completely flooded with water. The emotions and buzzing energy were cleansed. The receding water left a neutral room.

I was then at my seat at the table; in front of me were thrones. The center being told me that my soul had agreed to this moment—the moment that led me to the exploration of expression, self-assurance, and self-worth. This was my initiation into my soul's mission—to lose my confidence and rebirth it so I could teach others how to create the confidence they desire in their own lives.

In the spiritual realm behind that moment in my past, I could now see my higher self holding ceremony for my human-self concurrently with my physical experience. I now understand that the girl who had hurt me was fulfilling her soul's contract with mine. It was such an important moment to my soul that it resounded through my timeline, and an echo broke through to my consciousness early as my premonition.

I was never supposed to be able to suppress my true self. My natural personality is big and bold. At that moment, I *finally* stopped judging myself for these qualities. I'm outspoken, perceptive, energetic, passionate, bubbly, and—what I fought so hard to rebuild—confident.

Not everyone is comfortable with the energy of these qualities. I make some people feel uncomfortable; I'm annoying even. Some feel resentful to see me do what they've told themselves that they aren't *allowed* to do. Some feel inspired to embody more of who they are meant to be.

My wish for every woman is that she sees herself as wildly deserving of being herself. You aren't 'too' anything. You have always been sufficiently *enough* and equally as worthy as every other person.

3

IN FIRE

CORINNE SCHWERS

LINDA WAS AN INJURED woman. In turn, she injured her child, Felicia, who later injured her children, Tom and Celia.

Of Jewish descent, Linda fled from Belgium to France to protect her newborn child. Being Jewish was terrible during the war, as so many men, women, and children had to hide to avoid being sent to concentration camps.

Eventually, Linda learned via letter that her father had been sent to the gas chamber and, believing that she could have saved her father had she stayed in Brussels, she placed the blame and responsibility on her innocent baby in her pain and grief. Because of this belief, she experienced troubles with attachment and struggled to bond with her daughter.

In the years after the war, Linda was nasty to Felicia, neglecting her, denying her love, and not authorizing her to be herself. To receive her mother's attention throughout her life, Felicia felt she 'had to' become ill. Linda made fun of and humiliated Felicia; she did not consider her daughter's needs or desires. Despite her unconscious hatred for her mother, Felicia held back her claws for a long time, and evil was done.

In 1962, when Felicia married her husband at the age of twenty-three, they settled in the same house as her mother. They transformed the first floor, which was originally Felicia's apartment, into an apartment for the couple. One room, then two rooms were added later when the first, then the second child, came along.

She didn't exercise her right to go and live on her own with her husband because, despite her mother's lack of affection, she was still attached to her mother. Unconsciously, Felicia felt that she had to repay her mother to be 'forgiven' for her grandfather's death, even though it was not something she was truly responsible for. When she had her first child, she had trouble attaching to him and felt guilty that she was not able to 'properly' love her little Tom.

Tom became a gift from Felicia to her mother in an effort to seek forgiveness, while Celia, Tom's younger sister, became her own child to love. But Celia felt Tom's anxiety and became anxious herself. She was so afraid of losing the love of her mother, because she saw her brother being unloved, that she tried to be 'perfect' and to become what she thought her mother wanted her to be. Felicia overprotected Celia, which caused the little girl to feel humiliated, guilty, and as though she never measured up to the task.

Eventually, Celia grew up to become a young woman torn between loyalty and rebellion, trying to become who her mother wanted her to be; if her mother found her fat, she then became obese and was humiliated by her mother because of this. It was difficult for Celia to be angry with her mother, as she was in constant fear of disappointing her and not living up to what she thought her mother wanted. Her perfectionism often defeated her, and so, at twenty-two years old, even though she settled in a small apartment of her own, she did not escape the claws of her mother, on whom she was still unconsciously dependent.

In her social life and relationships, Celia sought the recognition of others—while hating the world. Her romantic relationships were brief, and she broke them quickly for fear of being tied down. Over the next thirty years of her life's journey, she embraced spirituality, then music, which helped her to understand *herself* better, but she was still unable to find a stable relationship.

The men she dated proved to be manipulative, humiliating, and often 'guilt-tripped' her. While she was with one particularly terrible man, Celia fell pregnant, yet gave birth to a son who filled her with joy and happiness.

When her son was fifteen months old, she met (and later married) a man she was interested in, but this relationship still only brought her suffering. The only truly positive thing that came from her marriage was the possibility of studying at university—a master's in geography—but this, however, made her sink into depression and alcohol in an effort to cope with her situation and feelings about herself.

A year or so later, Celia reached a point where she decided she needed to cure her negative thoughts and feelings. This journey brought a true and real awareness of herself and the impact her upbringing had on her life.

Finally, she decided to free herself, to escape, and to stand on her own two feet. She changed her life, settled elsewhere with her son, and began to treat herself with compassion, to heal, and to seek balance, a new job, and a new reason for living.

Astonishingly, it was after the death of her mother, Felicia, that Celia finally felt a shift that allowed her to take off and become herself. She searched for many weeks to find what she was looking for, but eventually found the help she needed, and finally managed to lift her head from under the water.

Through working on herself and beginning to understand how her life experiences had influenced her thoughts and beliefs, Celia became aware of her pains, even if they were not physical, and the inner, unconscious anger that eventually fell away.

After some difficult moments along the way, Celia finally managed to drop the moorings and found a goal in life that suited her. She knew it was important to create a job she loved, one that would help her become financially and emotionally independent. She started a business to help women digitize their coaching businesses, and little by little, she felt increasing inner energy as her life came into alignment.

Although some would say that, at fifty-three, it is almost the end of life, for Celia, it was the beginning.

4

CODED FOR SILENCE, DESTINED TO SPEAK: ONE WOMAN'S SEARCH FOR HER TRUE VOICE

Carolyn Parker

The Coding Begins

To be female, born in the late fifties, and the offspring of an unmarried mother was to begin life at the bottom of an invisible heap with shame as your middle name wrapped in a blanket of pity.

If a baby girl were to grow up to be a thought leader, she would not be the illegitimate daughter of a poor teenage girl made to scrub the stairs of the Mother and Baby Unit until her day of confinement.

Nor would she be the child of a father who was conspicuous by his absence both on her birth certificate and in person, thereby consigning her to forever search for, yet never discover, her ancestry—or so English law decreed at the time of her birth.

However, once 'adopted' was added to her identity descriptors, the chance of making something of her life stepped up a notch. She gained a degree of respectability from this transition, now being considered to be connected—albeit tentatively—to the upper middle classes along with her professional, thirty-something, adoptive parents living in their suburban, three-bedroom detached house, surrounded by their circle of bridge, golf, and theatre friends.

This 'fortunate' female, you may have guessed, was no other than myself, Carolyn Jane, not to be confused or compared with Patricia Anne (my pre-adoption identity).

I was, my new mother often told me, a very *good* baby, as I rarely cried. If only she had known this was not a sign of contentment but a survival instinct; that to be quiet was to be safe.

At three-and-a-half years old, I was sent to kindergarten, where I quickly absorbed everything the teachers put in front of me, together with a side of separation anxiety and the social expectations of the day. I wasn't the only adoptee, but I *was* the only single child amongst them, which increased my sense of not belonging and loneliness, despite being surrounded by my peers.

They say a child absorbs everything they hear, see, or experience without question up to the age of seven, accepting it as normal.

My normal was to be unwanted by some who saw my very existence as a threat that needed to be extinguished, yet I survived.

My normal was to absorb my mother's embarrassment, shame, and stress arising from her fear of being found out by her parents and employer.

My normal was the need to stay hidden, for to hide was to be safe, allowing my mother to avoid others' condescending looks and faces filled with judgement for as long as possible.

My normal was to be considered an object of pity, rejected and thought of as the product of sin; a devil's child, some said.

My normal was to be surrounded by a ring of compressed trauma, imperceptible to the naked eye of my longed-for playmates, who were repelled by its negative energy field, and which I unknowingly projected throughout my childhood into the later years of adulthood.

These inbuilt values and beliefs were encoded into the very fabric of my being from conception, determining, I believe, the way I thought about myself and behaved from my earliest days.

Adding Insult to Injury

How much of my reticence to give my voice free rein can be put down to the circumstances surrounding my birth, and how much I can attribute to the cultural rules and expectations of English society in the nineteen sixties to the early twenty-first century is debatable.

It is common knowledge that we are all, to some degree, the product of our environment. For me, that was patriarchal, with an unspoken charter of principles, rights, and wrongs that individuals and communities observed if they wanted to be thought of as respectable citizens.

These regulations determined how my family conducted itself, influencing everything from the length of my school summer dress, to the acceptable employment for my mother, to the way I was to address my teacher.

In polite society, small talk was the order of the day, with strict prohibitions on swearing and any talk of money, sex, religion, or politics.

Anyone who dared to overstep these by voicing ideas outside the accepted norm was simply shunned by the rest of the community. These 'outsiders' were viewed with suspicion, as they were thought to be likely to disrupt the group dynamics by encouraging others to think for themselves. They were not to be trusted and, therefore, were feared.

With such a litany of rules, I found myself, with my already skewed understanding of normality, leaning heavily towards silence as the best policy, joining the majority of other women and girls in toeing the line, unwilling to break the status quo.

We were, after all, living not so many years from the height of the Suffragette movement and were keenly aware of the fate of those women who had boldly defied the law of the land in order to stand up for the right of all women to speak, be heard, and vote.

To be seen and not heard as a child or adolescent was considered a virtue to be emulated. To speak out of turn was not. To do so would have my father telling me to 'button up' or 'zip it.' If I should dare to try to reply or explain, he would then tell me not to cheek my elders.

Chastened, I would pipe down and swallow my frustration at this seeming injustice.

And so it was that I grew up with my earliest beliefs around holding my tongue confirmed and enhanced.

I was to speak only when I was spoken to, or when it was my turn—and then politely. I was coded not to think outside the box, to be curious or creative when it came to opinions on what was deemed by society to be correct.

My conditioning was complete...

I was coded for silence

Many Years Later: From Silence to Resilience and Beyond

A person can only suffer so much in silence. At some point, they will break and rebel against a coercive and controlling hand laid against them in anger. No man or woman should ever be a puppet or rag doll in the grip of another's iron fist or will.

To refuse to resist at first appears to be the route to escape further harm yet, on an almost daily basis, I was thrown across a room, had my head pounded on a wall, or in some other way felt the wrath of my abuser, my partner, my captor. My skin was a canvas of blue, red, purple, black, and yellow pigments. My mind torn between strategising for survival and normalising my plight. My emotions pulled from love to hatred mixed with fear, hurt, and confusion.

Where was my voice?

As an unknowing victim of narcissistic abuse, my voice, opinion, and my very essence shrank into my core. Only carefully considered words designed to please or soothe my abuser were spoken.

I stumbled through many chaotic days plotting my escape as I lay on my mattress at night, yet any plans seemed futile, my energy being depleted by the necessity to stay constantly alert due to the unpredictability of each moment.

Looking back, I smile at my younger self's resilience and refusal to accept the hopelessness of the situation, unaware I was playing the role of willing victim in a cruel charade.

Yet, I did survive and escape, my self-esteem in tatters, my heart well and truly shattered, and my faith in mankind broken almost beyond repair. My love for life slowly returned, one smile and one kindness at a time.

Then it happened. Through a random conversation, I discovered the concept of having a growth mindset along with the benefits of applying personal development tools to my life. This new way of thinking reawakened an inner flame of hope and I set about rewiring my brain one affirmation at a time. The effect was incredible.

Within weeks, I was acutely aware of my inner critic and the origin of many of my beliefs. I was excited to realise I could change how I felt about myself simply by choosing a new inner dialogue. As a consequence of this reprogramming, my self-talk became more loving and my self-image improved. I was starting to accept and love myself.

Four years on and I am a completely different person. The old, fearful me, who berated herself at every turn, is gone and the new, optimistic me with a quietly confident attitude is becoming more apparent with every passing week. I love her.

I love her!

This expansive version of myself thrives on jumping out of her comfort zone, saying yes to aligned opportunities that light her up. She has faced and embraced her roots, working through her past pain to an extent where she is able to be a voice for those who haven't yet found their voice.

I am finally the fabulous, free woman I was always destined to be, standing tall and fearlessly speaking my truth.

I am a woman who has truly found her voice.

5

FLAMES OF HEALING

CHRISTINE FREY

MY PHONE RANG ON my birthday at 8:20pm. Answering, I heard my friend, a neighbor of my parents, say, "Chris, there's something bad happening at your parents' house right now and you need to come right away. Your mom and dad's house is on fire. You need to come now!"

Shocked, I threw on some clothes, telling my husband, Mike, that we needed to hurry. Driving as quickly as possible, we arrived at my parents' neighborhood to see fire trucks, ambulances, thick smoke, and ravenous flames.

As we drove there, I called my siblings and family members to let them know something bad had happened. Mike and I weren't allowed to pull up close to their house, so I told him to stop the car and I ran towards their house as fast as my legs could carry me.

The scene was eerily quiet and so surreal; I clearly felt the numbness of shock instantly wash through me. To my right was someone receiving

CPR in an ambulance, and to my left, I saw bystanders and police officers, some stood there watching the scene while others walked around. Confused and overwhelmed with shock, my run slowed to a walk as I saw my childhood home fully ablaze, flames pouring out of all the windows, doors, and roof.

A police officer stopped me to ask my name and determine my relationship with the people who lived there. When I told him that my parents lived in that house, his face changed. Frantically I looked around, trying to find my parents—and when I asked the officer where my parents were, he was quiet. Looking at the ambulance to my right, I asked who was in there. He responded with, "Your mother." Shocked, I asked if she was ok—and he said, "No."

Then I asked where my father was and he told me that my father was in the house and that they believed he was deceased as well. Suddenly I felt faint; Mike caught me as my legs gave out. This police officer explained that firefighters did go into the house to try to save my parents, but that they had to back out from the intense heat, thick, blinding smoke, and the imminent danger of the floors collapsing.

The neighbor who had called came over and hugged me as he cried on my shoulder. He was a volunteer firefighter, and when he saw the fire at my parents' house, he called for help before running over to help them. He repeatedly tried to open their front door but it wouldn't budge—and the fire was intensifying. Not giving up, he tried to get into the house through a window, constantly screaming their names, to try to save them.

One very brave firefighter went into their home using a thermal imaging device, and found my deceased mother on the second floor, hiding behind a bedroom dresser. Gently, he put her over his shoulder and carried her out of the house. Once they got outside, he gave her to the waiting paramedics who immediately started CPR.

My parents lived in a dead-end street and their property was full of trees and uneven terrain, however, one paramedic straddled my mother on the gurney to begin compressions as the others put leads on her body to try to find a heartbeat. They continued to do CPR as they carried the gurney down the steep, dark, rocky road towards the ambulance. Even though she was clinically deceased, they continued CPR to keep her organs viable for possible donation.

Their home was a three-hundred-year-old stone farmhouse with original wood inside and out, including creosote-treated floors and ceilings. There were no words to express my shock and grief as I watched my childhood home burn to the ground, the fire lighting up the night and pouring smoke high into the sky. News helicopters flew overhead, reporting their big news of death and devastation, and there were lots of sirens and flashing lights all around me.

Another police officer told me that two firefighters had gone into the house using their thermal imaging devices, and found my father's body lying in the middle of the heart of the fire. They said he was burned beyond recognition and they couldn't safely remove his body because of the safety risks to the firefighters.

Overwhelmed with grief, I turned and ran about fifty yards to an open field, where I instantly fell to my knees, put my head in my hands, and screamed. I kept talking to God, asking for help because I did not know how to survive this. I turned my face up to the sky and cried with heartbreaking sorrow and gut-wrenching, bone-deep anguish.

At that moment, everything around me became quiet and still, and I heard God tell me to stand up and turn around. When I did so, I clearly saw Jesus standing a few yards in front me near a line of trees. I will never forget the feeling of deep peace, calm, and serenity that surrounded and penetrated me. Just then, Mike walked up behind me, put his hand on my shoulder, and hugged me.

My husband and I left the horrific scene when we were asked to go to the local hospital to identify my mother's body. According to the coroner, my mother had seen, or heard, my father die, and she ran up the stairs to her bedroom and hid behind a small dresser, where she died of smoke inhalation amid the intense heat. Again, I called my siblings and family as we followed the ambulance to the hospital, tailed by a police escort.

When we arrived at the hospital, we were directed to the quiet room where heartbreaking news was privately delivered to family and friends. Some of my family were waiting there for me; the silence was palpable.

Then I was taken to a room where I saw my mother's body. She looked so beautiful and peaceful. The firefighter did everything he could to protect her as he carried her out of the house, and all she had was a tiny burn on her right ear and left shoulder. My father died instantly, and the coroner advised us not to view his body because he was so badly burned from being in the middle of the hottest part of the fire.

The next days were surreal as we began to deal with everything that had to be done after two people unexpectedly died. We all worked together to prepare for two funerals, organize the demolition of the historic house, and close out my parents' final affairs. There was not a lot left for us to salvage from the house, but we did find a few personal treasures.

Mike did the most work at their house, including sleeping there in his truck to keep vandals out. More than once, he ventured into the house to try to find us something to help heal our grieving hearts. The house quickly became moldy from the firefighters' attempts to put the fire out, and the burned floors were ready to collapse.

Three months later, Mike was diagnosed with Stage Four Larynx Cancer, which was exacerbated by the smoke and mold in that house. After many extensive surgeries, Mike was cured of cancer, however, my husband of twenty years died from end-stage liver disease and lifelong polysubstance abuse. We will never forget his selfless devotion to my parents' legacy and the work he did to help all of us to heal.

I have made many unhealthy decisions and choices in my life, and most of them were related to my relationships with my parents, ex-husband, and late husband, Mike. I grew up in a volatile, dysfunctional home where my father's excessive alcoholism ruled the house with fear and domestic violence. My parents had grown up in the same type of chaos—that was all they knew—and that was how I subconsciously learned to deeply ingrain these toxic traits of survival mode into my entire being.

I married a man like my father, and for twelve years I stayed in a highly dysfunctional marriage because all I knew was how to repeat the cycle of violence and trauma that was so familiar to me. During this time, my parents and I had a falling out where we didn't communicate for many years, due to the fact that I chose to stand by my ex-husband instead of my parents.

I didn't want my parents to see my marriage fail, that I was a lot like them, and that I had made a poor choice in husbands. My anger towards my parents was unfounded and my denial of the truth of my ex-husband's actions and behaviors prevented me from seeing my life as anything less than normal.

After my divorce, I met Mike and we quickly married and blended our families. Mike knew what had happened between my parents and me, and he immediately helped me understand that I needed to apologize and repair my relationship with my parents.

I was grateful to have them in my life again and to introduce them to their grandchildren for the first time. Spending time with my parents filled my heart with joy—and a longing for normalcy. My parents were more kind, gentle, and calm than I remembered, which helped me finally have the parents I always wanted and needed.

In time, I have worked through the self-doubt that exists around my memories and have validated my feelings and life experiences. It has taken a lot of work, patience, faith, and trust in all parts of myself: physically, mentally, emotionally, and spiritually. For forty-nine years, I thought I was content in 'survival mode' when, in reality, I was stuck in the dead-end cycle of despair, scarcity, and dysfunction.

Losing my parents shook me to the core, and I then began to learn so much about grace, forgiveness, and compassion for myself. While Mike was actively dying, I needed to give him all of my attention due to his early onset dementia, numerous doctor and hospital visits, multiple surgeries, and extended stays in the hospital.

Still stuck in survival mode, I began therapy sessions, holistic healings, and group therapies. Learning that, "I am not what happened to me" was quite liberating, and I was able to see more clearly that I was a survivor who endured many experiences—and came out the other side.

Seeing a glimpse of life without the burdens of labeling myself as anything less than a brave and courageous human being was startling! *Who was I to be so bold as to think I was deserving of peace, calm, respect, safety, and truth?* I questioned whether this was true when I realized there are people with healthy marriages and family relationships who have a strong sense of self-esteem, self-confidence, and self-love.

When Mike died, I was shocked by the concept of being a single woman for the first time in my life. Daring to step outside my comfort zone of the 'survival' model is when I truly started my deep and profound, life-changing healing. It was exciting and terrifying to step a toe into 'thriving' mode, because my mind kept filling with thoughts of, *Who do you think you are to do, and be, better than your parents—especially your mother?*

I felt disrespectful to my mother because I was doing what she always wanted, and was never able to. She never got free from an abusive marriage and domestic violence, and her life was stuck in survival mode until the night she died. I know my mother wanted to live a safe and productive life, but every time she tried to get a job or go out with friends, my father refused to allow her the freedom to do so.

Both of my parents were raised in violent, dysfunctional homes, and that was all they knew, so they mirrored those things to their children. Unfortunately, I raised my children in a violent, dysfunctional home that closely resembled my upbringing. There were many times I realized that this was not healthy for any of us, yet I stayed because I had the mindset that this was all that I deserved, all I would ever have, and that I, alone, was not capable of supporting myself and my family.

With thoughts such as, *It's better to stay here than out in the dangerous world*, and, *My kids need a roof and food today, so I will stay*, this short-term mindset clearly shows I was existing in survival mode.

But, in time, and with the right support, I refused to be a victim and someone who did not demand respect, decency, integrity and love in all of my relationships. Breaking the chains of my dysfunctional upbringing has taken a lot of hard work, sweat, and tears, however I have been extremely grateful for the soul lessons I have learned along the way. Although I have always been very spiritual, I recognized that my relationship with my Higher Power was on a contingent basis, and that I was not putting in the work to listen to Spirit. I was asking for things that were not meant for me, and I do thank God for the unanswered prayers.

I had been asking Spirit for things that were a huge part of my survival mindset, things that no longer served me as I began to step firmly into the "new me" in thriving mode. I learned about the need to "pause," to be fully present in my life, how to respond instead of react, and that I needed to create firm boundaries. *"No." is a complete sentence? I do not have to over explain myself to others? I can speak my truth and know that I am welcome to do so?*

Through my exploration, I discovered that this was my fourth life as a domestic violence and sexual assault survivor and that, because I was reclaiming, accepting, and loving all parts of myself, I was going to end this destructive cycle. I know we can not heal everything in one life, and when we come into our next life we may choose to learn those valuable soul lessons—or not. And every life that you do not learn the soul lessons makes the lessons more challenging. Spirit tries to get our attention; as human beings, we often think we have all of the answers to help ourselves, not realizing that we are standing in our own way and delaying our spiritual growth.

I have learned that when I chose to live this life, I chose the perfect body to move through life as the perfect home for my soul. Being in this body allows me to engage in life with all of my senses to constantly bring information into my soul. This information is meant to serve as a wealth of information about what Spirit truly wants me—and you—to learn in this life. For so many years, I allowed others to harm my body and I used it as a survival mechanism, a tool; I did not realize it is so much more than that. It has taken me many years to realize that my body is meant to be treasured, respected, and well taken care of.

6

THE BEAUTIFUL BRIDGE

Teri Katzenberger

Welcome to the third installment of our *Wounded Women Series*! I would like to begin by saying, "I am so flipping proud of you! YES! YOU!" We write FOR you! Our hope, my hope, is that every individual who reads our personal stories feel they are being heard, seen, and valued.

I share my personal life happenings—trials and tribulations, anguish and torment, mental, emotional, and verbal abuse, adult bullying, etc.—in the hope that you, the reader, can feel at ease knowing you are not alone on your own journey in this thing called life.

As you continue reading, may you connect with one of us (or several of us) on a more personal level, and that we are instrumental in helping you set yourself free from all the toxic ugliness in your own life. I am here to help you 'build' your Beautiful Bridge, as you set your own soul on fire for a more beautiful life ahead.

When people who have been mistreated use the term 'burned,' they are often describing the emotional or psychological toll of betrayal, manipulation, or mistreatment by others. In this context, being 'burned' goes beyond a physical injury and encompasses feelings of hurt, disappointment, and a sense of being deceived or let down.

You see, in my early years here on Earth, I overcame a grossly abusive marriage at the age of nineteen. I also overcame a chronic, life-destroying alcohol and drug addiction, and a chronic dual eating disorder that was killing me from the inside out. ALL at the same time. I had no one to turn to. Nowhere to go. No one who truly and honestly cared about me and my well-being, let alone my life.

Without my absolute faith and belief in a God who loves me *and* cares about me, I would not be alive today to share my life with you.

When I got clean and sober (finally) in April of 1991, I went to live in a halfway house for women: the Second Street Manor. Although I wasn't the only female in that house, I always felt like I was completely alone on my newfound journey in this thing called life. Not only did I feel like I didn't belong in the world, I felt like I didn't really have a place in this house.

My family had no interest in my life nor did they truly care if I lived or died. Just sayin'—that truth 'burns' in my soul. That is why I was where I was. In May of 1991, I honestly thought I had a loving family to go home to after I left the intensive drug and alcohol treatment hospital.

Having to make plans about where I would go when I was discharged after completing my program, I remember telling my counselor and the case worker during my 'exit' interview that, "I have a loving and caring family. My family loves me very much and really cares about me. They will want me home with them."

Little did I know, my counselor, Rose, and the case worker had already spoken to my parents—my family. My parents did not want me to come home. That means I went from a grossly abusive marriage, to jail, back to the abuser, back to jail, and so on—then four years later, I was admitted into the intensive treatment hospital.

It hurt to realize, "I am alive. I am safe. I am on my way to a new clean and healthy life. I survived a four-year nightmare at the hands of an abuser and now, I have nowhere to go. No one to turn to. A family who truly does not care about me or my life. I have a choice between a halfway house or a homeless shelter."

This experience paved the way for the person I would become. I was twenty-three-years-old. I give Thanks every day for Second Street Manor. It truly was instrumental in saving my life and helping me pave my way to a new clean and sober way of living. Finally, I was in a position to design my own new life here on Earth.

I am still friends with Mary Beth, one of the staff members there. Several years later, after I had left and was living on my own, I ran into this amazing woman in a local thrift store. I introduced myself and let her know how I knew her, then shared my experience of Second Street Manor and what an amazing blessing she was to me. I let her know how much she meant to me and how a day did not go by that I did not think of her and give God all of the Glory for her being a shining light and blessing to me in my newfound, fragile, and vulnerable life.

I bring up this particular chapter in my life as a reminder of the person I was becoming. I was empowered! Strong. Confident. On a mission to live my life for ME! Finally taking back all that the abuser and others had taken from me. My confidence. My voice. My well-being. My self-esteem. My God-given life!

I remember this time of my life as if it were yesterday. The moments leading up to finally graduating from Second Street Manor after a short six months; thirty-two years later, I still have the beautiful vase I received from the staff and the other girls who were living there. (I am looking at it right now, as it sits on my office desk.) My divorce becoming final. Saving enough money to finally live on my own. I was twenty-three. Alone and on a life-changing mission! Navigating into the big, real world by myself. Now an adult, I was lost! But I did it! And I have never looked back.

But there was one thing during this time in my life that I completely forgot about. A major part that forever changed my outlook on life, my attitude, my mission, and my future self.

I forgot about my personal life standards that I set for myself when I left the halfway house. I followed these standards from that day forward (in October 1991) and lived by them for the next ten years. It wasn't until recently—when I was flooded with my past self, that I somehow lost along my new-found journey—that I also lost my personal life standards.

My Personal Life Standards:

- *If you don't like the way I look? Don't look at me!*
- *If you don't like the sound of my voice? Don't talk to me!*
- *If you don't like what I have to say? Don't talk to me!*
- *If you don't like who I am? Stay away from me!*
- *I like who I am. Your opinion does not matter to me!*

This list of standards helped take back all that was taken from me over the first twenty-three years of my life. I stood by this with confidence, strength, and courage. I was becoming the best version of myself.

Why these particular standards?

You see, all through my upbringing, my mother never liked the sound of my voice, how I looked, nor did she like Me! A thorn in her side from the day I was born, I was programmed to believe that I was not good enough. I didn't 'look' good enough, my voice wasn't 'good' enough, my existence just wasn't 'good enough.'

No one cared what I had to say, what my accomplishments were, let alone how life was treating me.

The Lost Life

When I look back on my life, I can honestly say I have never thought of being 'burned.' It is not a term I would use when people mistreated, betrayed, or deceived me.

Over the course of thirty-two years, however, that is exactly what consistently happened at the hands of people I deeply loved, trusted, and cared about. People who are family. People I thought were close personal friends. And others who just like to be the pot-stirrer, stabbing you in the back as they smile and hug you from the front.

For some reason, along my journey—beginning in 2000 and moving forward—I completely lost the person I had become. Slowly, I lost my voice. My existence. I forgot about my Personal Life Standards! I began to lose sight of who I was and I let my guard down. I began to let go of my standards.

Little did I know, that is when I began to slowly die from the inside out.

Instead of keeping the fire burning in my soul, I began being burned from the inside out by the people I surrounded myself with. The very people I would have bet my life would always be there for me. The very people I thought would have my back, stand by me, and stand with me. For the next twenty-plus years, my life would never be the same again.

Burned [bərnd] ADJECTIVE

1. Destroyed, damaged, or injured

2. To insult (someone) in a particularly cutting way:

- When someone has "effed" you over

- Where someone disrespects or insults another person

- It can also be used to describe the act of making fun of someone or mocking them. The term is often used in a playful or humorous way, but it can also be used in a more serious or hurtful manner.

- When people betray you, deceive you, stab you in the back and/or belittle and mock you

Although it has been happening since the day I was born, in around 2015 my eyes became wide open to the mental, emotional, and verbal abuse from my mother. To this day, I have absolutely no idea what triggered it, nor do I know why. All I know is my mother had nothing to do with me ever again. She let me know what an uneducated, classless, rotten human being I was, and tried to lead me to believe that absolutely no one was for me.

As I stood before her listening to her hateful words, visions of people began flashing before my eyes. I looked at my mother and simply said, "You and the family do not have to be for me. That is ok. There are so many others who will always be for me."

I left her home on that particular day in December 2016 as she yelled, "No, you do not have anyone who is for you. No one is for you!" I knew then, that it would be the last time I ever stepped foot in the house I grew up in.

I was devastated but I never looked back. I did not allow her hateful words to destroy me. The visions of people who flashed before my eyes: THEY are the real deal! THEY are MY People! THEY are FOR ME! My Beautiful Bridge was slowly being destroyed one step at a time. Little did I know that the mental and emotional abuse would continue to torment me and cause me anguish for the next six years.

I am not saying this has been an easy road; it has caused me decades of harm.

When hurt is caused by your family, it becomes even more disabling. Every day, I lost more of that strong, confident, courageous woman by allowing the actions and words of others to paralyze me from the inside out. I was being destroyed. And only I knew it. I attended family gatherings based on 'how I felt,' not realizing I was slowly being plagued with overwhelming social anxiety and depression. My Beautiful Bridge was losing its edge.

Each day I stood strong and continued to be the person God created me to be. I remember the exact day when God revealed the purpose of my life. I needed to know, and had cried out to Him numerous times. I was being slowly 'burned' and just couldn't deal with the pain any longer.

The Holy Spirit says: "You are to walk in peace to love and serve His people." Since I received this message, every day I have done just that.

Now as I look back, I realize it was that exact moment in time where I stopped allowing anyone to 'burn' me. Meaning, life got harder, people became meaner, and the mental and emotional abuse from family and close friends escalated. However, I walked in peace, to love and serve all people anyway.

From 2016 into 2018, I was bullied and tormented by women I grew up with. A handful of so-called 'close' friends began to make my life a living hell. Why? WHO THE HELL KNOWS! You see, when you pick up the phone to 'call them out' on their abuse, they don't have anything to say. 'Burned' would be a complete understatement.

In 2016, we were all turning forty-nine and fifty years old! Their level of cruelty was disturbing. The mental mind games. The pot stirrers. The back stabbers. Women I loved with all my heart. Women I thought I would continue to form a stronger bond and enjoy life with! To go on adventures. To explore life in our fifties and beyond. TOGETHER!

My Beautiful Bridge was becoming shorter and more fragile, but I can honestly say that I did not allow them to break my spirit. Although the social anxiety was becoming more overwhelming, and paranoia was being added to the mix of the depression, I did not allow them to break me.

I stood firm on my Faith and knew that God still cares for me AND He loves me. I would envision those who flashed before my eyes in December 2016 and hang on to MY ABSOLUTE TRUTH! So many people are for me. So many people care about me and truly love me. For support, I'd reach out to my, now very small, circle of amazing friends.

My twin brother went to heaven in December 2020. When I allow people to live rent-free in my head I hear, and begin saying, his words, "Don't let the bastards run ya down!" and I laugh, and chuckle, and smile!

To Burn or Not To Burn the Bridge

When I think about being 'burned,' it reflects a profound emotional impact. It's like a breach of trust, with broken promises and deceit causing deep wounds. For me, the term captures lasting emotional scars that make it tough to trust again.

Experiencing exploitation or betrayal by someone you once trusted intensifies the pain and disappointment. This often leads to skepticism in relationships, where trust becomes a cautious endeavor. The emotional anguish can chip away at your self-worth, prompting a journey to rebuild confidence. Despite the pain, being 'burned' can be a crucial learning experience, fostering self-awareness and resilience in the face of challenges.

Feeling 'burned' by others has caused me deep, agonizing pain and anguish. Being let down and lied to, breaking the trust I had—or *thought* I had. Although it can make it difficult to trust again, I look at it this way: now I am more *cautious* with certain people. If I allow the actions of others to continue to alter who I am and *Whose I Am*, they have control over me.

I refuse to allow the actions of others to dictate who God created ME to be! I refuse to allow people to live rent-free 'in me!'

Although the emotional pain caused me to lose confidence, weaken my strength, and become less courageous, going through these years of mental and emotional anguish and torment at the hands of people I deeply loved and cared for has helped me learn more about myself. Slowly, I am becoming stronger, more confident, and getting my courage back. Facing difficulties has become easier, with less overwhelm and mental chaos.

I know we have all heard the sayings: "Be careful not to burn bridges," and, "You want to make sure you don't burn any bridges!"

> *Burn (one's) bridges: Literally, to destroy a bridge or path behind oneself, so that others cannot follow.*

'Burning bridges' is often used to describe the act of intentionally cutting off relationships with people or opportunities. It means to destroy one's path, reputation, connections, and opportunities. The phrase is particularly used when someone intentionally cuts off these relationships.

And I have to ask myself, *Is it really all that bad if I burn my bridge?*

We have to guard ourselves against those who are not FOR us. If people aren't 'for' you, they are 'against' you. People cannot 'love' you AND 'hate' you. That is not how this realm works. It is one or the other.

Again, I need to really ask myself, *To burn or NOT to burn the bridge?*

Let's explore further:

'Burn Bridges'—the Meaning

The idiomatic phrase 'burn bridges' means, "the inability to revert to an earlier state or position." In other words, 'burning your bridges' implies being forced to continue with a specific course of action, with no point of return, or the provision to reinstate the original.

Why would I want toxic people to have a point of return, or give them an opportunity to reinstate their life back into mine? *They* burned their own bridge. I, in all my faith and heavenly spirit, continued to keep the door to my bridge open. REALLY? Why would I want more abuse?

I was continuing to walk in God's purpose for my life: "Walk in peace to love and serve God's people."

I made a direct vow, "I do NOT have to act the way other people act. I do NOT have to treat people the way they treat me!"

Besides relationships, other things that can have their 'bridges burnt' include 'path,' 'reputation,' 'connections,' and 'opportunities.' Generally, the bridges that are burnt, or the connections, relationships, and so on that get wrecked, are done intentionally, and the actions are usually rooted in ignorance.

Simply, I have allowed the haters, the pot stirrers, the bullies, and their entourage, to crash and burn all on their own. There is no need for me to follow their path of self-destruction. They have a problem with *ME*. I never had a problem with *THEM*.

You see, we don't need to get 'vengeance.' I am not a person who believes in 'karma.' I walk in faith. I trust in God. I continue to be who HE created me to be. We don't always have to be on attack. Let people go about their own life leaving a burning path of hatred and discontent along the way—YOU do not have to!

Here's what I have learned, and why I take the road less traveled: It is far easier to live amongst the world and world views than it is to chart your own course and stay faithfully on your own magnificent path. Live by your own Personal Life Standards.

Most people don't want to see others succeed. Most people don't want to see others happy and living life to the fullest. As the saying goes, "Misery loves company." Well, it's no wonder I have always felt very alone in my world. I refuse to hang out with Misery! The smaller my circle, the more peace and serenity I have!

Now, Do NOT! I repeat, DO NOT begin rebuilding the bridges that others have burnt! If they do not serve you well. If they are not for you. If they do not genuinely love you—let the ashes lay. Our nature is to want to always reach out. We want everyone to like us. To be happy for us. We want toxic people to include us in their lives.

I totally understand your pushback on this. Please trust me: you do not need to be the one who rebuilds bridges that do not serve you and your future self well! Pain may come in the night, but joy will always come in the morning! Take it from me, a strong badass woman who continued to cross the bridges that led me back into the hands of the haters, pot stirrers, and bullies.

Do I think I wasted years of my life? You know it! That was another obstacle I have had to get over: not hating myself for allowing the actions of others to ruin so many days, weeks, months, and years of my life. You see, I didn't know that I was building my own Beautiful Bridge. I never realized that my original *Beautiful* Bridge was taking me *back* on the path of toxic evil destruction.

Life is a mystery. We may think people have burned their bridges where we are concerned, however, the truth be told, they will continue to allow us to cross 'back' on because *Misery loves company!* And when we stop crossing their toxic bridge to head back their way, they think WE burned the bridge!

Our absolute truth is: We are not responsible for another person's bridge, we are only responsible for our own mental and emotional health and wellness—our own Beautiful Bridge. When we choose to continue to live life *FORWARD,* they despise us for our strength, courage, and confidence, therefore, blaming us for 'burning bridges.'

Continue to live your life forward and let the haters hate. You have absolutely nothing to lose and nothing to prove!

Fanning the Flames and Burning the Bridge

The time has now come for me to begin to set my soul back on fire! To take back ALL that I have allowed the enemy to steal.

Fanning the flames of the fire within our soul is an art of self-discovery and passion. It's about nurturing the embers of our deepest desires and ambitions until they blaze with undeniable intensity. This inner fire propels us forward, providing warmth, purpose, and a guiding light through life's journey. It's a commitment to stoking the furnace of your dreams, allowing the radiant glow to illuminate your path and infuse every endeavor with the unwavering energy that comes from within.

There are Dream Stealers in our midst. I challenge you to become a Dream Releaser! Join me in fanning your flames to spark the fire within your spirit. Setting your Soul on fire! You deserve it! You deserve to be set free!

Here is what I have learned on my journey in this thing called life: when it comes to the haters, the pot stirrers, the bullies, they have no desire to be part of my life. Now, they may want to be 'in' my life so they can stay in the loop of what I am up to—therefore having something for the pot stirrers to mix around. The truth be told (by my experience), they do not truly care about me. They just want to be in the 'know' so they have something to gossip about, hate on, and a reason to bully me.

Sick? Oh, I know. And I am sure it is hard to believe. Trust me, the people—and my life happenings—are 100% real, raw truth.

As a close friend told me in 2016, "Oh I believe you. You just can't make this shit up"!

I realized that I needed to begin burning and REBUILDING my Beautiful Bridge. But not to prevent people from crossing onto my path, nor to keep people out of my life.

I had an awakening in October 2023 telling me, "You need to burn your bridge that paves the way for *YOU* to go 'back' to those who abuse, bully, and torment *YOU*! It is ok to burn your bridge that takes you on the path *back* to the toxic, hateful people who are not for you." I embraced that Holy Spirit-filled moment and thought, "DEAR LORD, YES!"

Sometimes it is ok to *'burn OUR bridge.'* Other times, it is crucial that we burn what is paving the way to destroy us. You see, I no longer need to pave the way for the haters, the pot stirrers, the bullies, and their entourage. I would be an absolute fool to continue to allow them onto my Beautiful Bridge and into my anointed life. Nor do I need to keep my Beautiful Bridge built to allow temptation to set in and pull me backward into the dark, toxic hell on earth. My Beautifully Burned Bridge is a masterpiece of strength, confidence, and courage.

Only the most determined will see the value in burning their bridge that continues to lead them *back* on the path of destruction and the lost life. You see, burning your bridge does not have to have a negative meaning. It truly can be your most magnificent moment in time—where you finally are able to set yourself free from all that is determined to destroy you!

This doesn't mean that I don't love my family and close childhood friends. It strictly means that I do not have to allow them to enter my life with hatred and discontent. I can love people from afar. I do not have to keep my beautiful path paved for *them*.

There comes a time, in this thing called life, where we have to love ourselves more than those who hate and despise us. Do not allow their noise to be louder than your voice!

Start fanning the flame within your soul and begin to put out the flames from those who continue to burn you. Let's reword that: Put out the flames of those who *ATTEMPT TO* continue to burn you. Put out the flames of those who have burned you in the past, yet you have kept those hateful, tormenting embers burning. I get it! I spent thirty years fanning the flames of people who continued to burn me. Hence the word, 'continued.' Had I known what I know now, I would have stopped fanning those flames a long time ago.

Knowing what I know now, I would have burned my Beautiful Bridge decades ago. But I have no regrets. I know that all things come in their own due time. I am stronger today. I am more confident today. I am filled with courage today. Today, they can no longer hurt me.

When I realized that I have absolutely nothing to lose, I felt myself being set free. That is why I openly share my story—because I have absolutely nothing to lose. The haters gonna hate, regardless, and I have absolutely nothing to prove! I owe evil nothing!

Building a New Beautiful Bridge

In September 2023, I experienced another awakening: "Do not reward bad behavior."

I learned a long time ago that people will treat you the way they feel you deserve to be treated. It's just who they are; some people are miserable, hate-filled people who do not have love in their hearts. I refuse to conform to them. I refuse to reward their bad behavior by allowing them to live rent-free in me, dim the fire in my spirit, and weaken the flame in my soul!

I refuse to allow them to step foot on the new Beautiful Bridge I am building. NOT *'rebuilding.'* It's important that we understand this; I do NOT want to 'rebuild' something that once was subject to hate, discontent, bullying, and toxic energy. I am on my own personal mission to build a brand NEW Beautiful Bridge with NEW Personal Life Standards.

You may be thinking, "UGH! This would be so hard to do. I'm not as strong as you. I don't think I could ever do this." I know exactly what you are saying, why you are saying it, and where you are coming from. My absolute truth is: IT WAS NEVER EASY for me! I have been on this mental and emotional journey since 1991, and instead of my life getting easier and more manageable, it became harder, unmanageable, lonely, scary, and disturbing.

There is only one thing that began making my journey more simple. I say 'simple,' because the bridges leading to haters, bullies, pot stirrers, and their entourage grew more toxic, more hate-filled, and more disturbing as each year passed. It was like I was 'white-knuckling it' through life as I knew it.

Although these people continued to fan their own evil flames, I hung on stronger to my faith and belief in Jesus Christ, who IS MY STRENGTH! I continued to live life forward! Doing my absolute best to NOT turn back nor walk back onto the burning bridges. It has never been easy—but it remains doable and well worth it!

So what was the ONE thing that made my journey more simple, that allowed me to finally exhale overwhelm, anxiety, paranoia, and depression, and inhale strength, courage, and confidence?

It was when I understood why Jesus left Nazareth, the town He grew up in. You see, even Jesus had family, relatives, and close friends who were not for Him. In His hometown, He had haters, bullies, and pot stirrers. He refused to stay where He was not wanted. He walked out of Nazareth, wiped his feet, and never looked back!

I encourage you to wipe your feet from the toxic ashes that you carry in your mind, body, and spirit. Walk forward onto your own Beautiful Bridge. No looking back!

HOMEWORK: Building Your Beautiful Bridge

1. Write out your own Personal Life Standards. Something that sings your song!

2. Take back your life! Do not allow people to destroy you!

3. Don't rebuild a burned bridge if it does not serve you well.

4. Start fanning your flame to ignite your soul on fire!

5. Do not reward bad behavior.

6. Do not allow others to live rent-free in your mind.

7. Do not allow others to dim the fire in your spirit.

8. Do not allow others to weaken the flame in your soul!

9. Build your NEW Beautiful Bridge!

10. Wipe your feet, walk away, and never look back!

I help women overcome hurts, habits, and hangups that prevent them from achieving their best, healthy, and happy self and life. I would be honored to meet you and have a personal virtual coffee talk with you!

7

BREAKING THE CHAINS: UNLEASHING MY VOICE TO RECLAIM MY POWER

Laura Rinnankoski

I HAVE ALWAYS LIKED to express myself. As a child, I was always talking, singing, and communicating with everyone around me. I'm aware I was always very different to the people around me, but I always thought that it was due to being so 'international' because I was born in Finland, grew up in Venezuela, and went to international American schools.

But over the years, I have come to realize that I have always been different because my soul has a higher calling. When I first came to Ireland, I remember an astrologer telling me that even if I had lived all my life in Finland, I would still be different—and that made sense to me. When your soul has a higher calling, the background of your life on Earth is secondary.

I have always known that I have a big mission in this life and that I am here to help people. When I was a child, I would ask my mom what the purpose of my life was—most kids don't ask these types of questions. An incredibly aware and conscientious child, I was also very happy and joyful. On top of this, I have always enjoyed singing, participating in school plays, and have done lots of writing and journaling.

The Tapestry of My Soul

I grew up in Venezuela, a South American country where women are encouraged to look pretty, but are not encouraged to speak their truth. Venezuela takes beauty—and beauty pageants—very seriously, which is reflected in the fact that this country has won the most beauty pageants in the world.

When women express themselves, it tends to be in very dramatic ways, as portrayed in Venezuelan novelas or soap operas. In the old-school way of thinking, men are smart and rational, and women are pretty and dramatic.

Finland, my birth country, views women in a very different way: Finnish women are very strong and speak their truth. One of the reasons for their strength is due to the many wars that have been fought. While the men were fighting in the wars, the women took care of everything that had to be done.

In 1906, Finnish women became the first in the world to have unrestricted rights both to vote and to stand for parliament. Tarja Halonen served as the eleventh president of Finland and was the first woman to hold the position—from 2000 to 2012. In the nineties, I met her in Caracas, and swam with her when she was a minister; little did I know at the time that I was swimming with the future first woman President of Finland!

Finland is the third most gender-equal country in the world. Finnish women have embraced their power and view themselves as equal to men. The third female prime minister of Finland, Sanna Marin, was instated in December 2019. At that time, she was both the world's youngest current state leader as well as the youngest-ever prime minister in Finland. Curiously, the first Miss Universe, in 1952, was 'Miss Finland,' Armi Kuusela.

The two countries I consider my home countries, Finland and Venezuela, view women in a very different ways. In Finland, women are encouraged to be strong and speak their truth, and in Venezuela women are encouraged to look pretty and not be very vocal; to stay quiet. Having grown up with both influences, it has been challenging at times to find the balance between my two worlds, and to find the right way to express myself in all ways.

A Love that Pushes You to Your Limits and Beyond

When you have a big mission, sometimes people will come into your life who will challenge you to your core to see how serious you are about this mission.

In my life, a person like that taught me big lessons about staying true to myself and speaking my truth. When we first met, things were good and harmonious between us, and we focused on the things that we had in common.

After a few months, things started to change, and he started saying negative things to me; at first, it was subtle, then it became blatant. The change was gradual and significant at the same time, and I began to notice that it coincided with me getting more visibility and acknowledgment.

When you are a strong woman with a big mission, you want a strong man by your side who will support you and take you higher. If a man is scared or intimidated by your success, then he is not the right partner for you.

A Journey from Silence to Empowerment and Freedom

Recently, during an Akashic Records reading and healing, I discovered that I had made a vow of poverty and silence in a past life. (I know that there are people who believe in past lives, and people who don't believe in past lives. Whatever you believe, is your choice. It is not my intention to convince you about anything. I am here telling you my story and you can draw your own conclusions.)

In that life, I was a young boy training to be a monk, and I had to take a vow of silence and poverty. A vow of silence works when you are training to be a monk—but not when you are an International Transformational Life and Relationship Coach with a big mission to help people!

Even though I took this vow two lifetimes ago, it was still affecting me. Vows can impact us across time and space, and across many lifetimes. When I heard about this vow, I was ready to break it—so I did!

It felt very powerful and cathartic to break this vow, and to make space for a new stage in my life full of expression and abundance in all ways! I feel like I am doing all the talking in this life that I did not do in that life.

In the past year, I have become a bestselling author, received six awards, and appeared on four magazine covers, so I am very visible now, which confirms that the vow has definitely been broken!

The Sacred Union

The energies on Earth are out-of-balance right now, and I feel it is very important to find a balance between the feminine and masculine energies. We will find that balance by listening to each other, respecting each other, and letting each other speak. It's not about the feminine energies becoming stronger than the masculine energies, or not needing the masculine energies—it's about finding the divine balance in both. We create divine partnership in the New Earth when our empowered divine feminine and divine masculine come together harmoniously.

Overcoming Fear and Embracing Your Authentic Voice

Several times, I have been told to be quiet and not speak my truth. The old version of me would obey and not say anything, but the new, empowered version of me stands in her power and speaks her truth!

No matter your background, or your background story, always stay true to yourself and speak your truth. It is so important for people to have the courage to express themselves and be heard.

We all have a song inside us waiting to be expressed, so don't leave this Earth with that song inside you. There are many ways you can express yourself—through talking, writing, singing, dancing—find what works for you and stay true to yourself in all ways.

There are moments in life when we all get Burned, but the important thing is that when that happens, you don't stay in that Burned place. You dust yourself off, learn what you need to learn from that experience, and then move on—stronger than ever!

8

PHOENIX RISING

Tara Haislip

In *Broken,* the previous book in this series, I touched on a major shift I had experienced. During this shift, I began to remove my dance career from my life, mainly due to how emotionally painful it all felt.

I'd like to take a moment to honor my younger self and all of her accomplishments.

By the time I was twenty-one, I had performed with numerous artists as well as worked with various choreographers and artistic directors that included The Rock School of Dance, Philadanco, Junk, Brandywine, Pennsylvania Ballet, The Martha Graham Dance Company, and Liverpool Institute of Performing Arts (LIPA). I did all this while in school and working full-time, and graduated from the University of the Arts with a Bachelor of Fine Arts degree.

By the age of twenty-two, I had completely changed my career path to become a paralegal. My paralegal career kicked off with a job as a student clerk at the Department of Justice, United States Attorney's Office, and ended in a specialized area of Estate Planning law as a Trust and Estate Administration paralegal.

Then, six years later, at the age of thirty, I decided that Corporate did not fit the healing version of myself, and I became an entrepreneur.

When I outline all that I have accomplished in my young adult years, it looks pretty impressive. It also looks like I changed directions on a whim. There was a reason, however, for each transition. I struggled with each career development and went through a lot of shadow work to find internal, as well as external, peace for each career growth.

The Shadows

I spent six years in Corporate, looking for myself. During those years, I dove deeper into my healing journey—emotionally and mentally—while at the same time trying to find that perfect job that provided everything: good pay, schedule autonomy, and career advancement. But I kept hitting financial and career advancement ceilings.

Even though I had the house, the car, and the soon-to-be husband, there was no money left at the end of every pay period. I would have to use a credit card to cover basic expenses like extra gas, groceries, or increases in utility costs. At this realization, I started to assess the life I was building and asked myself if it was what I had envisioned.

No. It was not what I had envisioned for my life. Between the mortgage, car payment, student loans, and credit card payments to offset what my income didn't cover in basic expenses, I was more in debt than when I started. So I decided to consciously dismantle and rebuild my life the way I had desired it to be.

In 2017, I left my paralegal career, sold my house, and started over. To bring in some income, I got a job at a local marina while I figured out the what and how of building my own business.

About eight months later, I left the marina to work at a local resort spa, as well as working three other jobs to try to make ends meet. This is when I became pregnant with my first child.

It was an extremely difficult time, but I kept going, believing in myself and my vision for the future. I dove back into my spiritual practice to help keep me grounded.

Believe me, there were many days I questioned what in the actual fuck had I done. I went too far on investing in my business with credit cards. I was drowning. I was hiding it from my husband. I knew I had fucked up on the financial piece.

By 2020, I was exhausted. In August of that year, I invested in working with a recruiter who combined mindfulness tools with traditional career coaching tools. I was getting lots of interviews, but no job offers. By October, I was beginning to doubt my break would come.

Then, one Saturday morning when I was lying in bed staring at the ceiling, circling in my thoughts, I happened to look at my phone notifications. There was one job post that stood out. I looked into the job as well as the company and decided to set it aside because I thought it would be another dead end.

But something about it kept nagging me to apply. The following Monday, I applied—and then forgot about it.

A week or two later, I received an email inviting me to an interview, which I scheduled and attended without getting my hopes up. Then I received a second interview invitation, and then a third. By the third interview, I had hoped that this would be my break.

It was. I was selected as one of forty in this new company's first round of major hires and I couldn't have been more excited. I was chosen not only for my coaching background, but also my entrepreneurial background. This job gave me everything I had been looking for—good pay, schedule autonomy, and the ability to work from home (WFH). I felt like I could breathe for the first time in three years. By March 2021, I was full-time and my little family was able to take our first vacation. I was able to afford my bills and living expenses. I was building savings and a retirement fund.

By August 2021, I was chosen to be one of a team of first-round managers. At this time, my husband and I were looking at buying or building a home and starting to talk about having a second child. Thankfully, we were able to celebrate the holidays without the stress of where we were going to get the money to afford the holidays. My little family and I were starting to heal.

The Phoenix

In January 2022, I felt called back to my practice, which was odd considering how well things were going at work. I did, however, sense some cracks forming in conjunction with sudden leadership changes that had occurred at the end of 2021. I didn't give it too much thought as the new leadership wanted to keep the community and collaborative workplace culture intact. So I decided to listen to my intuition to slowly start to explore reigniting my business.

By August 2022, I no longer recognized the company I worked for. The cracks I had seen had turned into fractures. The work culture that was once about community and collaboration had become a traditional corporate culture with people stepping on anyone they could to get ahead. It was a daily mental battle. Every day I logged on, I wondered if I would still have a job by the time I logged off. Every day I logged off, I would breathe a sigh of relief that I still had my job.

At the same time, my family lost our rental due to a structural issue. We moved in with my in-laws while we figured out if we wanted to buy or build our home. I knew my job was no longer stable. The idea of committing to a mortgage made me extremely anxious. On top of all of that, we were pregnant with our second child.

I struggled to believe the Universe would give me all of this stability only to take it away. But, then it happened. It was at the beginning of my second trimester when I, with the rest of the organization, was pulled into a mandatory meeting. I remember feeling numb and thinking, *This isn't fucking happening right now*. Sure enough, I was laid off in the middle of the holiday season—pregnant, and (essentially) homeless.

This time, the Universe was in charge of my life breakdown. I could either go with the flow, or fight it and struggle. If I had learned anything from my past, it was that the more I fought, the more I struggled. So I buckled up and started to go with the flow, which often meant doing nothing. This time, I knew I had to let life events unfold without me getting in the way. It was very difficult to be still.

I mourned for the future I thought I was advancing towards. I mourned the loss of not only my job but all the healing my little family had experienced. I mourned for the new life within me who was experiencing all of my emotions, which meant they were experiencing everything no different than if they were earthside. Many nights, I cried. I retreated within myself. I dove into my business to help me find consistency in the chaos.

Now that I'm on the other side of this breakdown, I see that the Universe has my back. My last job was the Universe's way of giving me a big, deep, breath before plunging me into the depths of my shadows for a massive course correction that brought me the very things I had been envisioning for my life since I left corporate.

So, now, like a Phoenix, I begin to rise from my ashes, to fully live the vision of my life dreams.

9

THERE'S MORE TO LIFE THAN JUST FISH

Jennifer Arwen Templeton

There are a thousand and one ways we are burned: a friend or lover, our parents or job, our choices, or thinking this one more time will be different, and yet, the abuse still comes.

This often has me asking: What if the source of our pain comes not just from this life but also from the lives we have lived before? Surely this amount of darkness is more than one life can bear?

Among the things I miss is never experiencing those adult conversations with her; the family secrets and the womanly advice that don't come when you're just a kid.

I also miss the memories of him. Now only faint echoes and forgotten dreams. Only hope can conjure such happiness, yet I have none. Hope, love, and the dream are just out of reach—gone forever. I can still feel the comfort of his arms and the absolute knowing that this was meant to be. The last place I felt safe, the last time I felt joy.

Happiness? Sure, but that's the thing about healed wounds—buried decades ago, they're still there, beneath the surface. It becomes easier to wear the façade, but the grief still grips my heart and clenches my lungs as if it were yesterday. "Young love doesn't last," they say and yet, to this day, he remains the love of my life, gone before I turned eighteen.

How can loss and grief exist with the feelings of betrayal, being broken, and burned? For me, it's this most unusual life of mine that has been slow-roasted over the fire of survival, of never belonging, of my closest family and tribe being on the other side, beyond the veil, without me.

The forging flames of the crucible is a place I know well, a place I return again and again, the place I am unsure I will ever leave. I know there's more to life—there's more to mine for certain—but it's the pain most easy to focus upon that leaves those scars, and letting go is impossible when the story of who you are is branded on your soul in a way that can't be fixed, only survived.

They say what doesn't kill us makes us stronger. I've had it with the universe conspiring to make me the next Hercules. Wait, he's a hero, right? Yeah, I'm more like Atlas then, carrying around the weight of the world simply because I seem incapable of setting it down. Of saying, "No more," of saying, "Enough."

When being burned is all you know, how is it possible to step out of the ashes? How do you rise from survival mode, and believe you deserve a better life, when a 'better life' is as foreign as a fairytale and the flames feel more like home?

Recently, after sharing the deepest of thoughts and exploring obscure topics, I mentioned to a longtime client of mine that I thought about starting a podcast called *The More*. I'm always looking deeper—curious, and unsettled—knowing there is more to life than just fish. Like Alice in Wonderland, I have six impossible ideas before breakfast.

We laughed and then I shared 'the fish story.' After the tears, there was laughter as she turned to me and said, "So you've always been like this!" She's known me for twenty-five years, and here she was saying the simplest thing—and a light turned on. In that moment, I recaptured the young woman who desired freedom and longed for adventure, even when her life experience had been more than most could survive.

Let's skip the abusive marriage and go back with her. Back to a time when hurt still held hope and grief fueled desire to live out loud.

My backstory in bits...

When your mother is killed and you're just eighteen months old, the trial-by-fire begins. Add to my story the 'Cinderella' ingredients of a father who checks out and becomes the shell of what he might have been, then makes the grave mistake of marrying for lust, not love, and definitely not for his children. He's never wanted 'the more,' he's completely fine with getting by and staying hidden behind his hurtful jokes that keep me at arm's length. I get it. I do.

By my age, you begin to forgive and see the classic story behind the personal scars, bad choices, and regret. I've come to peace with my life—I think, as tears slide down my cheeks. These hot, weeping tears have no real emotion or drama, just a sadness so deep that they well up, roll out and, like always, I wipe them away and move on.

The archetype of the stepmother: Wicked? Perhaps. Naive, juvenile, and emotionally stunted? Yes! I believe she didn't set out to be the wicked stepmother, yet that is the story my brother and I lived. Calling her by her first name. Knowing very well she never wanted kids; we were reminded often enough.

In answering my eight-year-old daughter, she said, "No honey, you call me by my first name because I can't be your grandmother. I've never had kids." She was clueless as to how that landed for me as I saw the hurt in my child's eyes. Clueless that I was standing right there, and she is the only mom I have ever known.

I was born in 1969, my mom died in 1970, and by 1972, my thirty-two year old, widowed father married a twenty-year-old who met her new 'step-children' only once before they walked down the aisle and into a life of turmoil.

We all come to relationships with our own baggage, and see life through our particular storied-lens. It's from this place we choose, we learn and, with any luck, we grow. I often tell my clients that you can love and learn from the past but you absolutely cannot live there.

My stepmother does, though. She rents a condo on the corner of Feel Sorry For Me Street and Same Old Story Boulevard. I do feel sorry for her, and for my father, but this is *my* story and the fire has taught me that no contract in life need be forever, even that between ourselves and our parents, or even our children.

I teach that there are three ways to navigate a broken relationship: One—Shift it. Two—Heal it. Three—Leave it. But that story belongs in another book series. One most likely named *Holy Shit, I've Made a Bad Choice,* and subtitled, *Too Burned To Know Better.*

Today, I choose to heal the relationship I have with myself.

Where am I going with all this talk of growing up a motherless daughter, always seeking 'the more,' ever curious about life? While so much runs through my mind to share with you, I'm unsure if my unquenchable curiosity is a gift, or a side-effect of keeping the focus away from myself.

I won't downplay the decades of study, personal development, spiritual questing, and the constant desire to know more. From wondering which came first—the hummingbird or the tube-like flower—to what happens when we die. I want to know 'the more,' or at least philosophize in my mind and talk late into the night with other lifelong students of the Universe.

Maybe that's it! Maybe it's not a flawed way of being, to not look at myself, but the fact that I've been burned so damn badly makes me incapable of talking about the everyday small stuff.

Okay, let's get to 'the more' that burned and 'the more' that's still burning…

Imagine the very late 1980s. Some close friends and I are standing in Long John Silver's fast food restaurant. It's near the end of my Senior year of high school. I can't tell you what Nancy, my best friend, and I had been doing earlier that night but I can bet it had to do with cruising, drinking, and random guys.

I, obviously, didn't have the best role models for healthy romantic relationships and, at this time, I didn't have anyone who cared where I was, or what, or who, I was doing.

Months earlier, my grandmother, my mother's mom, had been my everything and she would have kicked my ass for my behavior.

Months earlier, I would have been with him instead of staring aimlessly at the fast food menu sign.

However, this night she wasn't there to say… and he wasn't there to love… so here I stood broken, betrayed, and burned—and thinking about fish.

Two years prior, I was at my grandmother's in Missouri. As a little kid, I lived with her for years after my mom died and, as I grew older, I spent months there every summer. This one summer, I fell in love and while he and I connected more deeply and forged a bond beyond space and time, my grandmother was slowly losing her battle with breast cancer.

Unhappy at home, I asked my dad if I could stay there and live with her. Knowing she wouldn't be around long, I think he understood, but I know this request broke him more than I cared at the time. Until then, it had been my brother and I against the world but falling in love and living the dream was an easy choice as my brother was leaving for college and I would have been alone.

Two years went by; they were absolute bliss, occasionally tempered with bitter-sweet moments as my grandmother moved back and forth from home to hospital. Derrick and I had each other; his family became mine. His brother became like a brother to me and his little sister quickly found a place in my heart, one she keeps to this day.

It was this family who were there for me when the pain of being a motherless daughter went from imagined grief to excruciating reality. It was his mother who called the house that afternoon.

I assumed it was him. He was late. We had a date—a date that would never come. His father and sister picked me up on their way and, together, we drove to the hospital, hoping and praying but not knowing what to expect.

He breathed his last about the time I stepped through the sliding doors. It was a car accident on his way to pick me up.

Time became irrelevant. I couldn't tell you what happened during most of those days and weeks, other than I stayed with his family while my grandmother was once again in hospital. I slept curled in his bed. Broken.

After his funeral, my grandmother was able to come home and we had this moment where I couldn't stop crying and all she could do was pat my leg and say, "This is just like your mommy, this is just like your mommy." She knew my pain, although I didn't grasp that until I had children of my own. Sitting with me that day, the pain she remembered must have had her reeling back to the time her daughter was driven under the back of a parked bus and ripped from her life in an instant.

Months later I was set to graduate, and most likely move back to Georgia with my parents because one month after Derrick was killed, my grandmother died as well.

I quickly learned—the harsh way—that the grandfather I grew up with was truly my step-grandfather. I knew this but after the ties were broken and I wasn't really family anymore in his eyes, his eyes turned to the fact that I was a pretty young girl living under his roof. I had to get out. That betrayal still burns.

I feel like one of those commercials that shares a ton of information and still says, "But wait! There's more!" For now, my continued story of love, loss, death, broken, betrayed, and burned will have to wait for another day, another podcast, chapter, book, or story around the fire with my sisterhood of women who, after being beaten down by life, continue to thrive beyond all expectations.

I see you, Dear One, and you are not alone. Together we indeed rise… even when we crawl through the glass, time after time.

So I will wrap up with the fish story. I stood there in line with my friends, and one of the menu choices was 'Fish And More.' I turned to my friend,

Nancy, and said, "I think I'll get that because there has to be more to life than just fish."

That girl is the one I seek now, and I will pick up where she left off.

Before the haze of grief, bad choices, and survival mode, there was a young woman who saw glimpses of possibility through the veil of heartbreak.

The young woman who wanted to grab the backpack, head to Ireland, and see where the road would take her. The young woman who was free-spirited, untamed, and unconventional. The young woman who saw creativity and profound meaning in the most mundane of places. The woman I was before buying into society and being burned even more by ticking the boxes of school, career, marriage, house, kids, and death.

Let's see where this road goes... after all, there's more to this life than just fish.

10

THE QUIET REVOLUTION: FINDING MY OWN VOICE

Jamila Ekkel

Going Against the Grain

"Are you absolutely sure about this...?" My mother's eyes reflected a deep, genuine concern. She worried about leaving behind a child who, in her later years, might be alone without the support of her own offspring. At the time, this topic felt like an attack; it triggered a deep-seated discomfort within me.

"Mom, please stop. Let's not go here again," I responded sharply, a rush of defensive energy coursing through me. "I can take care of myself. And who knows? Maybe I'll meet kind people in the future who will want to help when I'm old. I'll manage..."

A sigh of relief followed, marking my first step in standing up for myself. But this initial triumph was quickly overshadowed by guilt and self-reproach. *I shouldn't have snapped like that*, I thought, regretting my harsh response to my mother's well-intentioned concern.

My focus shifted rapidly from asserting my boundaries to maintaining the role of a compliant daughter, ever eager to please.

For much of my life, I exerted great effort to conform to various roles: the dutiful daughter, the exceptional student, the model employee, and the caring girlfriend.

My existence was governed by an unwritten rule: Always abide by the rules, for they exist for a reason.

This adherence to societal norms and expectations meant that I consistently dimmed my own light, never allowing myself to stand out, whether for good or ill.

It wasn't until my early thirties that I realized I had never fully embraced my true power. Despite believing I was 'different' for my abstention from smoking, drinking, or drugs, and my propensity to forge my own path, I had never fully acknowledged all the facets of my identity.

As a human being, I am very introverted, meaning that I recharge my energy mostly from spending time on my own. Or at the most, through connecting to other people one-on-one. Groups of people wear me out entirely.

For years of my life, I couldn't reconcile with these parts of myself. I judged myself harshly—I thought I was 'boring,' 'too distant,' and even 'non-social.' Not surprisingly, these judgements were derived from societal expectations.

Western society is simply more focused on extroverts and promotes extroverted behavior. Group gatherings are being pushed everywhere!

Continual anxiety and layers of fear held me back all this time, preventing me from fulfilling my potential to inspire and motivate others by speaking my truth and embarking on a soul-healing journey.

These kinds of deep-seated wounds within our souls can be profound and multifaceted, emerging unexpectedly in various forms. They often dim our light and slow our progress on the path our souls are meant to tread.

The Journey to Self-Expression

The fear of speaking up and the anxiety of being rejected for who I truly am have been constant companions in my life. This fear resided in the darkest corners of my mind, a place where I lingered for way too long.

As a psychologist with over a decade of experience, I can confidently say that this fear of 'social rejection' is not unique to me. It's a deeply human fear, ingrained in our psyche to avoid social exclusion and protect our emotional and biological well-being.

Our society and generational norms condition us to withhold our opinions—to blend in, rather than stand out. I've lost count of how many times I've heard the saying, "If you don't have anything good to say, don't say anything at all." If I had a dollar for each time, I'd be super wealthy by now.

We humans, as a species, often engage in a subtle manipulation of each other in an attempt to control the social environment. This is a power struggle—not always conscious but, nonetheless, very real.

Eventually, I grew weary of this endless cycle. I was running on a societal hamster wheel that led absolutely nowhere and left me profoundly unhappy as I, however unintentionally, suppressed important parts of myself and denied my true nature.

For a while, I pondered why the opinions of others about my choice not to have children should matter to me. Also, why should their feelings about my introverted nature, and my need for solitude affect me? They were not living my life; they didn't possess my body or my introverted nervous system.

I don't need their permission, I once told myself with newfound confidence.

Convincing myself through affirmations, however, was one thing; fully embodying this newfound confidence was another. My 'awesome confidence tactic,' borrowed from Cognitive Behavioral Therapy, required more than just thought—it demanded action and practice.

But there was a problem. I was utterly exhausted with the way I was living. My patience had evaporated, and dark thoughts clouded my mind more than ever before. I was losing myself and needed a change, urgently.

It was then that the Universe seemed to answer my call. During my journey in business, I 'accidentally' encountered a woman who would become my trusted business energetics mentor and a dear friend. She introduced me to the world of spiritual energetics and energy healing, two concepts I initially approached with great skepticism.

My background in science had made me close-minded about anything that didn't fit into a logical, empirical framework. Science had, up until that point, been my safety net, providing control and predictability.

Yet, my worldview began to shift dramatically, aligning with the very change I had sought. This shift wasn't just a change in perspective; it was a transformation in how I saw the world, others, and, most importantly, myself.

Defying Gravity

In the musical, *Wicked*, Elphaba found power through her own outsider status. Her popular song, 'Defying Gravity,' is all about feeling scared of losing love and being rejected. And because of that fear: *keeping yourself small*.

Years of being a social outcast have formed Elphaba's low self-esteem but, later on, she decides that enough is enough and she is now willing to be wicked and *embody being the outcast*, if it means she can do good in the world.

Don't you think it's funny that her nickname is the 'Wicked Witch of the West?' (Witch Wound, anyone?)

One of my most profound beliefs actually touched on this topic. It entailed that people would abandon me once they discovered my true self. Overcoming this belief was absolutely crucial for my well-being and self-acceptance. I, too, had to come to terms with my own 'inner social outcast.'

My journey to this transformation was utterly unconventional. It wasn't through Cognitive Behavioral Therapy (CBT), meditation, journaling, EMDR, psychotherapy, EFT-tapping, or hypnotherapy. Being the scientist that I was, I had tried and tested all of those methods before, but the real, big, change occurred through deep energy healing—specifically by addressing a past life where I was a shaman, the healer and medicine woman of our tribe.

In this past life, I was an introverted young female shaman. Interestingly, my introversion wasn't the issue here, as many in the tribe were introverts. My behavior, however, was deemed 'different' and I didn't quite fit in because I used to communicate with animal spirits and plants, and dance under the moonlight beside a crackling bonfire.

Quite simply, I was highly misunderstood. My past self, apparently, had a profound connection with nature—a connection I had lost in my current life. So then why would I want to connect with life *or with myself* when, in that past life, I had been shunned and ostracized by my tribe? My soul had learned that it wasn't safe to be connected, which led to a pattern of disconnection in subsequent lives.

Writing this, I feel a sense of sadness for what I missed during all of those lives. And yet, there's also gratitude for having uncovered and released this core belief into the realm of unconditional love, healing the pain and resentment of my past self, and shedding all judgments.

Now, I am free. Free to be myself, unapologetically.

We may often hear the phrase "Be yourself unapologetically." While your logical mind might agree with this sentiment, your soul might hold a different belief. On the surface, you may nod in agreement, but deep down, unresolved issues might still linger.

Whether you're an introvert facing resistance, someone hesitant to voice strong opinions, or a business owner not attracting your ideal clients, I encourage you to delve deep into your soul. Start your journey to understand why certain patterns repeat in your life.

While these answers often involve interactions with others, it's important not to see ourselves as victims of their actions. People may attempt to gaslight, manipulate, diminish, or dim our light, but we simply do not have control over their behaviors. And you are the only one who continues to suffer.

A New Path of Self-Discovery

Healing from my past life has been a transformative journey that has enabled me to accept myself fully, including my introverted nature and the conscious choice to live without children. My healing process has also awakened a spiritual side within me, one that was previously inaccessible, leading to the revelation of a whole new world.

This discovery marked a significant pivot in my career as I transitioned my business into a more spiritual domain. Moving away from my role as a psychologist, I embraced a path that aligns more closely with my innate strengths and abilities, as opposed to only my acquired skills. Science, once my guide to understanding the world, has now taken a backseat to my intuition.

I perceive intuition as a powerful tool that compiles and processes vast amounts of external data and information, leading to quick and often accurate conclusions, sometimes even bypassing conscious awareness.

As we evolve as individuals, our intuition grows alongside us, especially when we work consciously to eliminate fear.

Fear, in my experience, is a formidable enemy of intuition. It's cunning, often disguising itself as a protective mechanism, yet it holds us back from achieving our deepest desires in life and business. It keeps us confined, inhibiting growth, regardless of its nature.

At the root of every fear, there lies a core wound—be it the 'Witch Wound,' a past life trauma, or even an experience from this lifetime. Fear always has an origin, a starting point, except for certain innate fears like acrophobia, thalassophobia, arachnophobia, or claustrophobia, which are more deeply ingrained in our human psyche.

When you've been subjected to silencing, exclusion, and gaslighting over the years, self-doubt becomes an inevitable consequence. This is a common experience for many, influenced by time and societal conditioning, and is often echoed in our past lives. Our souls remember these experiences and harbor a fear of separation from other souls, despite 'separation' being an illusion.

Our human experiences accumulate, life after life, making it increasingly challenging to trust the Universe and maintain our connection with our divine selves. We begin to identify more with our earthly selves, our egos, and consequently, our fears. Recognizing and addressing these fears is essential in our journey of self-discovery and growth.

Closing Thoughts

The fact that you are reading this book might stem from your curiosity about the 'Witch Wound'—what it is and how it manifests. Perhaps you're seeking to understand how it appears in your own life.

I hope my words have positively contributed to your search, and guide you toward your unique soul path, wherever it may lead.

I wish for you to find the courage within to confront your fears, no matter how they present themselves.

Remember not to let others dim your light; it's meant to shine brightly. Decide now to reclaim your power. It all begins with conscious awareness, and from there, we progress.

The next step involves delving into the subconscious fears and barriers that hinder your journey and mission. I invite you to take a moment, close your eyes, and breathe deeply. Contemplate these questions:

- Why can't I trust the Universe?
- Why doesn't it feel safe to fully connect with people?
- Why can't I fully speak my truth?

And for entrepreneurs:

- Why can't I attract more clients?

Shadow questions are here to help us find beliefs that are hidden deep within our subconscious—beliefs that influence us in our daily lives, sometimes in an unhelpful, or even self-sabotaging, way.

These shadow questions aren't necessarily 'the truth;' it might be that you actually do feel safe to connect to people. In that case, that's awesome! Many people, however, don't feel safe *with a lot of things* in life. And honestly? If you find yourself not yet achieving your goals, chances are that there's a subconscious belief bugging you. Big time.

Be open. Simply notice the answers in your brain. Allow yourself to explore and expand upon the stories behind these responses.

We all have stories, both positive and not-so-positive. These narratives, however, are often façades; constructs we maintain for safety and control. They don't define us, though we frequently believe they do.

Accepting this reality can be challenging. I've experienced this struggle firsthand. *Who was I beyond my stories? Who was Jamila without the labels of being an introvert, empath, good daughter, reliable friend, diligent student, or successful business owner?*

My journey wasn't about shedding these stories completely but about expanding my awareness and releasing the fears tied to narratives that no longer served me.

We don't need to abandon our identities entirely—we are still human. But it's crucial to let go of the stories, especially those linked to larger-scale generational wounds like the Witch Wound, that no longer serve us or society.

As we do this individually, we collectively raise our frequency—plus, we make the world a better place for the generations to come.

Healing ourselves and releasing our fears empowers us to speak up and share our truths more openly, thereby inspiring and motivating others.

My contribution to this book is a testament to this growth. Only a few months ago, I wouldn't have imagined sharing these insights because I was hindered by shame and the fear of judgment.

Will they accept my past life as a shaman? Will they understand my choice not to have children? These were fears I had to work through. This chapter, and my contribution to this book, marks a significant milestone in my personal spiritual journey.

Some experiences are life changing: this most certainly has been one of them. I am forever grateful for this opportunity to speak my own truth and release my story out in the world. Who knows who it might help?

Whether you are an introvert facing resistance, someone hesitant to voice strong opinions, or a business owner not currently attracting your ideal clients: I encourage you to delve deep into your soul.

Start your journey to understand why certain patterns repeat in your life. Everything happens for a reason. Know that every pattern has a core foundation. While these patterns most often involve interactions with others, it's important not to see ourselves as victims of their actions, even though *it can definitely feel that way.*

People may attempt to gaslight, manipulate, diminish, or dim our light, but we simply do not have control over their behaviors. Remember that *you* are oftentimes the only one who continues to suffer. You deserve better than that.

As Mahatma Gandhi wisely said, "You must be the change you wish to see in the world." Embrace this truth and start your journey of self-discovery and transformation today. Any day of your life is a good day to start.

With love, Jamila - Energy Healer (& former Psychologist)

II

THIS WITCH WON'T BURN

Tracey Brown

As a woman, have you ever been labelled 'too' anything? Too loud, too bossy, too intense? I know I have.

For a very long time, I tried to make myself smaller, more 'vanilla,' more mainstream. Less controversial, less opinionated, less of myself. Looking back now, it seems completely ridiculous to have twisted myself inside out to be what others wanted me to be instead of allowing myself to stand in my truth.

Hindsight has the benefit of time and knowledge that wasn't available to us, in those moments, while we were living them, though.

Use Your Inside Voice

While I was growing up, my father worked in airline management, so we had opportunities to attend events, travel, and meet all kinds of diverse people.

I recall my dad telling me that it was important to be *diplomatic* and not express controversial opinions—especially in a business context—because you never knew what the person you were speaking to believed, particularly when it came to religion or politics.

I remember often being told to use my 'inside voice,' something that continued to plague me throughout my career, as my bosses (usually the men) told me that I needed to be quieter and to calm down.

Over and over, it was both subtly and overtly drilled into me to keep my mouth shut, and my opinions to myself. Words, oh so many words, stuck in my throat, choking me as I held them back. I felt silenced and frustrated, and full of rage at my inability to be open and honest and speak my truth because to do so would be 'inappropriate.'

I became a master at 'people-pleasing,' learning to defer and deflect away from expressing any real opinion of my own—except when I knew it was safe. Sometimes it was a balancing act when I encountered people or conversations I disagreed with, as I tried to find any inch of common ground that I could latch onto without having to compromise my own beliefs.

Little Girls Making Play

Before I was conscious of any of the social conditioning to come, one of my earliest memories is of sitting at home in my sandpit, aged somewhere between three and five years old, mixing up sand and water 'magic potions' in little Tupperware containers.

One particular day, I took my little potion inside and dumped it into the kitchen sink, blissfully unaware that my mother had something cooling in there. My mother, meanwhile, watched in helpless horror as I unknowingly destroyed the dessert she was making for a dinner party!

I also spent many hours making magic potions at my Nanna's house with my brother and assorted cousins, using leaves, Lilly pilly berries, and water from the backyard hose.

One time we convinced one of our younger cousins to try the potion, but ended up being 'caught' by one of my uncles before she could actually drink it. To be honest, though, it was for the best—the men in my family were heavily into motor racing and it wasn't uncommon for containers that had contained motor oil or other toxic liquids to be lying around, and incorporated into our playtime.

Even from a young age I believed in magic and, despite having been on airplanes constantly and never seeing evidence of their existence, I was convinced that Care Bears and the land of Rainbow Brite existed somewhere in the clouds. I spent oh-so-many a night wishing on stars, and praying for signs that magic was real.

Don't Step Outside The Box

My family was more of a casual, Christmas-and-Easter-style churchgoing family, partly because of the frequency with which we moved and the time it took for my parents to find a suitable nearby church to attend. They were never 'bible-bashers,' but Christianity was a subtle and constant presence during my childhood and teen years.

At thirteen, while I was at boarding school, I bought the first issue of one of those multi-issue magazines that came with a selection of what I didn't know at the time were tarot cards. I was intensely curious and wanted to know more, but it was made clear very quickly that these cards were something 'dangerous' and not to be messed with.

I kept them in a shoebox for a long time, wondering what the big deal was... how could some pieces of paper with drawings on them be dangerous or invite in negative influences?

It was also during my time in boarding school that I started 'rebelling' against Christianity in general. Sitting through long sermons during assemblies, and reading the Bible in religious education classes just highlighted things that didn't sit well with me—not that I could put a finger on why, at the time.

Looking back it's super clear that the constant demonisation and degradation of women as unclean, impure, or wanton, and the promotion of patriarchy, in general, was already pricking at the edges of my awareness.

I continued to be intrigued by the esoteric, and when movies like *The Craft*, and *Practical Magic* came out, they quickly became fan faves.

Looking back as I write this chapter though, I can see how even 'progressive' movies like these (for the time) still upheld the warnings and the messages that *witchcraft=dangerous* and that bad things happen when you play with magic.

Don't step outside the box, girls, or bad things will happen to you.

Solitary Practitioner

At sixteen, I met a man named Peter who read tarot cards. We moved in mutual circles, and whenever I bumped into him at parties, I would hang around, fascinated, as he read cards for anyone who was interested.

He gifted me my very first tarot deck a short time later, telling me that it was bad luck to buy your first deck. I loved it then, and some twenty-odd years later it still holds pride of place in my collection.

It wasn't until I was in my late teens and very early twenties that I felt called to dive deeper and stick my toes in the spiritual waters. I found online witchcraft forums, had reiki sessions, booked regular aura soma massages, and invested in a growing collection of witchy books. I met some local pagans and a few of us formed a short-lived gardening group/plant swap, the Gardens of Avalon.

But as adventurous as I felt, I only shared that side of myself with those in my circle that felt 'safe' to come out of the spiritual closet to.

Still, I tried to let a little bit of it infuse into my daily life. I was interested in herbalism, and started growing herbs in pots on my balcony. I put all my books, cards, and magical items on a shelf together, albeit in a closet, instead of hidden in a box where no one could see them.

Around the time I turned twenty-one, my mum shared that she was worried for me because I was getting involved with things she didn't really understand. I assured her that there was nothing to worry about, but my confidence faltered with her perceived disapproval and I took a step firmly back into the closet.

At the turn of the millennium in Perth, Western Australia, Wicca, witchcraft and paganism were definitely not mainstream, and it went without saying that these were things best kept to oneself.

Don't let your freak flag fly where anyone can see it, okay? After all, it's not appropriate in a corporate setting, and you don't want it to affect your chances of getting a good job now, do you?

The Unwritten Rules Of Womanhood

Despite all the work women did through the early part of the 20th century to bring about equal rights for women, and the rise of feminism in the 1960s and 70s, while I was growing up in the 80s, 90s, and early 2000s, social conditioning around women's behaviour and place in society was still strong, if unspoken.

Yes, women could now have any job—in theory, at least—but our voices were still not as valued or as important as those of the men around us, and neither were our wants, needs, desires, or even the sovereignty of our bodies.

The biggest irony is, in my opinion, that the bad things that happen to women are almost always because of patriarchy, not because of witchcraft. But we all love a little bit of gaslighting, right, ladies?

This is the problem because, at that time, we didn't really have a voice or the power to say 'no.' There was always an ongoing war within as I tried to navigate the unwritten rules of being female:

- Be grateful for any attention you get, but don't put yourself in the spotlight or you're too brazen.

- Don't say no or you'll upset people—even when it makes you feel uncomfortable.

- What you want doesn't matter, be a good girl and do what you're told.

- Don't complain, you're lucky to have (insert thing here).

- You get what you're given, but don't you dare ask for what you want because you'll appear ungrateful and entitled.

- Always defer to your elders, especially when they're men, because they know better than you do.

And so, I did my best to stay quiet, blend in, do what I was told, and follow the path that was laid out before me.

I finished school and got into university to study a degree I was moderately interested in, even though I fantasised about being able to go to TAFE and study fashion design—a course that I got into, but *why on earth* would you *choose* to go to TAFE if you could get into university?

I got a summer job that turned into my first full-time job, bought my first apartment at eighteen, and my first new car at twenty-two. I had 'romantic' encounters—some I was into and some that I was ambivalent about at best.

By the time I turned twenty-five, I was a stay-at-home mum, following in the footsteps of all the women in my family who had come before me.

Get Back In Your Box

If I hadn't already been halfway back into the closet, having kids was enough to completely slam the door closed on my spirituality for a while.

Becoming a 'responsible' mother meant putting away 'childish things' like tarot cards, and frankly, I was too overwhelmed by running around after my young family to have any time to devote to myself or my interests.

But while my spirituality had entered a dormant phase, another part of me was awakening. One of the luxuries of being a full-time mum was that I was able to immerse myself in their activities.

Over the next few years, I stepped up into different community roles: becoming Playgroup leader, volunteering as committee President for their pre-Kindy classes, bench manager for their tee-ball team, team manager for their hockey team, sewing costumes for ballet recitals, joining the steering committee for the local community garden, and training to become a Cub Scout leader.

But despite all my activities and the purpose that had driven me in my home life, when I finally went back to work after my youngest started school, I felt like I'd been 'left behind' when it came to my career. Seven years out of the workforce meant that everyone I knew had climbed several rungs up the ladder while I'd dropped down because now I was only willing and able to work part-time.

I wanted more. I wanted to *be* more. I wanted to *achieve* more. But it felt like all the doors for advancement were closed to me because I was a *woman with children*—the worst kind of employee.

To be honest, I never really understood that philosophy, because women with children are penalised in advance for the perception that they'll be unreliable when really they've demonstrated that they can not only 'manage a team' and multitask but also, they demonstrate unfailing loyalty and commitment to a role.

By the same token, I'm also aware that *women without children* are also penalised in the workplace in other ways, often being expected to work the undesirable hours or over holiday periods because they 'don't have a family waiting at home.' Once again, patriarchy prevails and fucks women over either way.

Even though I demonstrated flexibility, adaptability, and a willingness to upskill in different areas of my work, I felt stifled and couldn't break through the glass ceiling—once again finding myself being told to 'use my inside voice' and calm down.

It didn't seem possible to have it all, but something inside me wanted to make a bigger impact and leave my mark on the world.

I started exploring other career options, trying to find a way to increase my income and move up the ladder, even within the confines of my part-time availability, which is when I discovered coaching. It was like flicking a light switch—something inside me just knew that this was a perfect opportunity for me to harness all the skills I had in a way that made sense.

However, I encountered resistance on the home front, and my decision to pursue coaching became a constant source of conflict in my marriage. In fact, over the next few years, I entered a period of struggle as my inner knowing became louder and impossible to ignore, while the people-pleasing side of me tried to maintain the status quo and attempted unsuccessfully to conform to the expectations of who I was, had been, and should continue to be.

Divine Reawakening

It was also during this time that my then-husband and I made the decision to relocate overseas to Italy, to pursue a dream of travelling the world and giving our children the opportunity to connect with the Italian heritage passed down through my mother's side of the family.

As I packed up our lives in preparation for the move, I de-stashed anything and everything we no longer needed to keep or take with us into our new life—including, for the most part, my witchy books and supplies.

After all, they hadn't been in use for years, and I felt like I was a non-practicing anything. The only things that made the cut were my two tarot decks and a couple of books that I couldn't bear to part with for sentimental reasons. Even though I kept them, I truly felt that much as I was shedding my old life in Australia, I was also shedding the 'witch' within.

Oh, how naïve I was!

Moving to Italy was like coming home, in ways I had never imagined. The shift in the pace of life, the slowing right down, allowed and encouraged me to ground myself into the seasonal cycles. It was like stepping into flow, and it was beautiful.

I felt deeply connected to the divine clock as it swept me along, anchoring in moments of pure love and joy like sparks of light that filled me with gratitude. Gratitude became the keystone to reconnecting with my intuition and feeling the whispers and nudges of my soul as it started to reawaken.

I felt drawn to explore my spirituality again, to reconnect with my tarot cards—including offering my first paid readings online.

Despite my rekindled interest, I actively rejected the idea of *needing* ritual or spiritual tools, shying away from the term 'witch,' and leaning heavily into the perspective that as the power flows through *you*, as a channel of the Divine, the tools themselves were just a conduit for the magic within.

While I still believe this to be true, in the sense that *we* are the channels, I no longer reject the rituals or tools as being irrelevant—they aren't *necessary*, but they allow us to amplify and shift into the mindset and mental space that aligns us with the vibrational frequency of what we wish to manifest.

For some, that shift in mindset and frequency is the very thing they need to access and channel their magic in the first place. So while I firmly believe that one doesn't *need* rituals and tools to be magical, I can appreciate that everyone's mileage may vary, and I'll be the first to admit that I *have* brought back rituals and tools into my own practice simply for amplification of intent.

The Old Ways Just Don't Work Anymore

The COVID-19 pandemic coincided with the completion of my first year in Italy, the launch of my coaching business, the onset of perimenopause, and my fortieth birthday. It was the perfect recipe for transformation: messy, full of drama, and chaos.

I had just run a Visionboarding Workshop and launched an in-person *Life Coaching with Wine* program in my local expat community in Torino when we found ourselves in lockdown. I was lucky enough to be able to transition my clients into working together online, but clearly I needed to adapt and evolve. So I made a hard pivot into online coaching and had to learn everything from the ground up.

It didn't take long for me to realise that 'bro marketing' wasn't for me. The idea that I needed to agitate pain points to heighten anxiety and play into a potential client's fear of missing out (FOMO) in order to convince them to work with me made me feel icky and gross. Surely there had to be another way?!

Something inside me resisted hard, and it was a relief to discover the concept of attraction, or lighthouse, marketing, where I could focus on making authentic connections with people through my content rather than forcing myself to fit into the 'hustle and grind' business paradigm that was prevalent at the time.

I invested in programs with coaches who embodied this energy, and found myself surrounded by like-minded women (and a few men) who also felt the need to do business 'differently.' This was my introduction to the delicate dance between masculine and feminine energetics—not male/female in a gender context, but the archetypal masculine (logic-driven, analytical, hustle, 'left brain,' yang, sun) and feminine (intuitive, flow, nurturing, 'right brain,' moon) energy.

The more I allowed myself to lean into the Divine Feminine, the more aligned I felt. The easier it became to express myself, and my thoughts, and my beliefs.

I was still playing it safe, though. I was afraid 'to be seen' by people I'd worked with in the past, afraid of what they would think of me, afraid to be seen as unprofessional—a joke. So I was 'out and proud' in spaces that felt safe—just as I had been twenty years earlier when I had explored my spirituality in my late teens—and completely closeted in spaces where I felt vulnerable and at risk of judgement.

Still, the more time I spent surrounded by 'the right people,' the more I felt called to speak up and speak out. It was harder to stay silent on issues that I disagreed with, and I often felt a blockage in my throat that burned.

I started researching the chakras, and discovered that the throat chakra is linked to our ability, or inability to speak our truth.

That a blockage in the throat chakra can manifest as an issue with sinuses (omg yes, I was struggling with the worst hayfever and sinus infections of my LIFE), tight shoulders (something I've always struggled with—I was always the girl who would get a massage and five minutes later my shoulders would be hunched back around my ears as if the massage had never happened), sore throats, upper respiratory infections, depression, anxiety, and low self-esteem—just to name a few.

Check, check, check. Hmm. I recognised that I had a blockage and that I needed to work on using my voice *more*.

To have hard conversations, the kinds that I'd been tamping down and shying away from so as not to upset the apple cart. Only, it appears the apple cart was rickety, and falling apart, and the silence I'd been keeping physically grated so hard that I could no longer keep my mouth shut.

The old me was falling away piece by piece, and a new me was emerging whether I liked it, whether I was afraid of it, whether I was ready for it, or not.

Stepping Out Of The Spiritual Closet

One of the first shifts I made in my business was to pivot away from the standard goal-setting-based coaching program I'd been using, and infusing elements of vision boarding, intention setting, and soul alignment into my methodology.

I wove in gratitude and forgiveness practices—the sames ones I'd been using to shift my own mindset as I worked through the self-doubt and impostor syndrome that plagued my entrepreneurial journey.

The second big shift, the catalyst, as it were, was discovering Moonology. I'd stumbled across Yasmin Boland's *Moonology Oracle* in an online tarot group and immediately felt a connection with the cards, however my bias against purchasing card decks for myself ran deep and I was convinced that if I was meant to own a set that the Universe would find a way to deliver them to me.

That might sound wildly optimistic, but if you've read my chapter, *Master Manifestor,* from my first collaborative book project, *Aligned Leaders* (which incidentally is where Jenny and I first crossed paths!), then you'll be familiar with the story of how I managed to manifest both the *Moonology Oracle* and Rebecca Campbell's *Work Your Light Oracle* decks within months of each other—along with a one-on-one personal destiny reading with Yasmin Boland herself.

If I'd been looking for a neon sign to indicate whether I was on the right path, it couldn't have been clearer. I was a *master manifestor*, and tapping into my intuition and spirituality was the key that unlocked the doors to a greater sense of purpose and fulfillment than I'd ever dreamed of.

Not only was I already practicing and teaching gratitude and forgiveness in my coaching, but the added dimension of aligning intention setting with the New Moon and forgiveness with the Full Moon just made sense.

It provided structure and accountability even though it also allowed intuition and the natural, rhythmic cycle of the lunar energy to lead the way. It was the perfect balance between masculine and feminine energetics.

Further confirmation came when Yasmin released her Certified Moonologer™ program a couple of months later and it wasn't even a question of whether I should sign up—I was a full-body HELL YES right from the get-go. It was time to take a leap of faith, surrender, and allow myself to realign and restructure my business without constantly second-guessing myself.

Letting The Witch Be Seen

I completed my certification on January 1st, 2021, and immediately started offering Moonology readings.

It felt completely natural to be living in harmony with the flow of the moon, and my business started to flourish (albeit slowly but surely!). I was starting to attract and work with my *dream* clients, and opportunities to collaborate with other women in business came my way too.

By late Spring of 2021, I was deep into the planning stages of a joint program creation with another divine lunar lady I'd become friends with in another program, and it felt wonderful to be co-creating a way to showcase different ways to work with the moon.

We started running weekly 'moon phase rooms' on Clubhouse, which was all the rage at that point in the pandemic, and I felt energised when I was surrounded by a group of other passionate moon practitioners, sharing our different interpretations, thoughts, beliefs, and experiences.

Unfortunately, over that summer, my almost-business-partner and I drifted apart. She felt called in a different direction, and we agreed to shelve our Circle of Wisdom program and circle back a few months later to see where we were at.

I kept running the Clubhouse rooms on my own, and in July I received the intuitive nudge that it was time to finally take the plunge and contribute a chapter to my first collaborative book project—the aforementioned, *Aligned Leaders*.

The witch within had been slowly infusing herself into my daily life in subtle ways. I'd fallen in love with ceremonial cacao, my witchy books had migrated their way onto the bookshelves in the living room where they were in plain sight, and I was creating New & Full Moon crystal grids on my 'bookshelf altar' that incorporated intention setting and forgiveness elements.

Past The Point Of No Return

I was no longer hiding, exactly, but I was still cautious. My then-husband and my children made fun of my witchiness, often casting me into a role that felt more like a caricature that they could ridicule.

All jokes aside though, the more openly I embraced my inner witch, the more the friction amplified in my marriage. He hated 'the moon shit,' calling it charlatanism and fortune telling. It was embarrassing, he said, and he was certain people felt sorry for me. There was nothing to be proud of in what I had achieved so far, or where I wanted to go.

Somewhere along the line, I had become a changeling, and he was unprepared for the outspoken, openly witchy, fiercely feminist woman who had taken the place of his predictable, diplomatic, socially acceptable wife.

I couldn't go back this time though, I couldn't undo what had been done, or step back inside my box. And frankly, I didn't want to.

What I wanted was to write, to speak, to share my story and my voice and my wisdom, and leave a legacy.

I wanted to set a good example for my daughter. To show her how to live unapologetically, and make sure she knew that it was okay to pursue her own dreams even if others couldn't appreciate it.

And so I wrote my chapter in *Aligned Leaders*, and launched my Moon Manifestation Academy membership off the back of the book launch, running fortnightly New and Full Moon circles.

I went on to write three more chapters in another three books in quick succession, and within 12 months of saying 'yes' to *Aligned Leaders*, I'd become a four-time international bestselling author.

To add salt to the wound, or perhaps more accurately, frosting to the cake, inspired by the Clubhouse rooms of the previous summer I decided to launch my publishing house, Gemini Moon Press, and its debut title, *Lunar Wisdom: Reconnecting with the Lunar Cycles Through Rituals, Spells, Magic, and the Phases of the Moon*.

I wanted to recapture the essence of a group of women, coming together to share their wisdom and their magic, and showcasing the different ways it was possible to work with the moon—that there was no one 'right' way. And for the most part, I achieved exactly what I set out to do.

It was, however, quite possibly the straw that broke the camel's back in my marriage. He approved of publishing in general, and in my decision to provide back-end publishing support to other indie publishing houses, but when it came to facilitating my own project—and a witchy one at that—I was taking it one step too far.

Realigning With The Whole Self

I've spent most of my life second-guessing every decision I've made, and lacked the confidence to stand in my convictions because I was constantly trying to weigh up what the best options were to make *everyone* happy—even if it meant I had to sacrifice what I wanted for the collective good.

The more aligned I became, though, and the more I gave myself permission to 'be selfish' and choose what was right for me and my business without apology, the more confident I became in myself, and the more certain I became about my mission, my purpose, and my vision for the future.

It would be dishonest to admit that I don't still have my moments where the 'Witch Wound' rears its ugly head and I feel an overwhelming desire to light a match, walk away, and burn everything to the ground when things get too real, too hard, or too scary.

But I've learned to acknowledge where those feelings are coming from, and let them wash over me—to feel the feelings, and then release them out into the Universe with love while focusing on what I want to be calling and anchoring in instead.

Part of realigning my whole self involved reintegrating all the different facets of myself that I'd previously kept separate. To accept my strengths as well as my weaknesses and challenges, and to practice radical self-love and self-acceptance.

I had to believe I was already enough, exactly as I was—not waiting 'until' I was something else. To stop seeking external validation while denying myself the internal validation that had the power to create a truly epic self-transformation.

The other part of realigning with my whole self was accepting what wasn't working—dismantling the unsustainable, and having the courage to let go.

In the end, I realised that I couldn't continue to stay in a relationship where the love was conditional, and where I was only worthy if I could manage to live up to the expectations set *for me* rather than *by me*.

It was no longer an option to twist myself out of shape in order to fit someone else's template of who I should be because the bittersweet truth is that I can only be me.

Me, in all my gloriously messy, imperfect facets. Shining my light unapologetically. Speaking my truth and standing tall, no matter what anyone else thinks.

And honestly, can I let you in on a little secret?

We often hold ourselves back, dim our light, and deny ourselves the things we really want, dream about, and desire because we have this belief that we're not 'allowed' to do things a certain way. That there are rules that cannot be violated and consequences if we do.

But here's the thing... you need to ask yourself *who* is it that's going to enforce these rules and consequences? Who says you can't have or do those things? Is it a real barrier, or just social conditioning not to colour outside the lines?

I can't speak for everyone else's individual experiences, but in my own experience, I discovered that what was really holding me back was me, and the prison in my mind.

Once I finally acknowledged to myself that my marriage was no longer serving either of us, that neither of us was challenging the other in constructive ways that encouraged us to become better people or push ourselves to achieve our goals and dreams, it became less scary to take the steps needed to push past the fear of breaking the rules and be honest about the fact that we were no longer a good fit.

It became easier to advocate for myself, and my kids.

But the most beautiful part of realigning with my whole self was that by choosing me, I opened myself up to new opportunities, in my life, in my business, and in my relationships.

By showing up as myself, in all my glory, I allowed myself to be fully seen and fully appreciated for all that I was bringing to the table. To be fully supported, and fully loved—*unconditionally*—by someone who doesn't think I'm 'too much,' but rather, that *I'm exactly enough*.

So for all you ladies out there, who like me, have ever been told that you're 'too' anything: let this be an invitation for you to realign with *your* whole self, throw off the shackles of society's expectations, and give yourself permission to shine beautifully bright in ALL your facets.

You are exactly enough, just as you are. xo

12

Unraveling the Witch Wound

Stephanie Moyer

If you are familiar with my work, or have read the first two books in the *Wounded Women Series*, then you know my childhood wasn't the best. Could have been worse, but it could have been better.

I ended up leaving home as a teenager and made my way through life the best I could, with tons of struggles, but also many triumphs.

In my early twenties, as a single mother and fresh out of an extremely abusive relationship, I met someone I connected with on a professional and mental level. We both wanted big things out of life: a successful business, nice cars, big homes, and complete financial freedom. He was intelligent, nice looking, had great manners, and was no stranger to hard work.

This man quickly became my hero. He understood me and accepted me for who I was through all my faults. We worked hard together and in early 2001, after living together for almost two years, we decided to take a chance on a failing business.

I uprooted my entire life and left all my friends and family to move a couple of states away to start anew. We struggled a bit in the beginning, as it's not easy to turn a business around, but we did it. In a very short time, we ended up transforming that neglected business into a multimillion-dollar corporation with two offices and over a hundred employees on our payroll.

But something was always missing. It felt like a hole I couldn't fill, no matter how successful we became.

It wasn't until I left my husband and that life that I noticed how suppressed and controlled I was. I didn't realize that I was living my life to please those who were important to me.

Before we moved away, I had gone back to school to finish a law degree. At that point in time, and because of a particular experience, I felt called to work in Family Law.

Despite being a single mom and working full-time as an office manager, I was doing great at school and had a 3.8 GPA. Then one day, the men I worked with, and for, called me into the office to discuss my career choice. They explained that my business was exactly where I was meant to be, that finishing my degree was going to be very difficult for me as I progressed, and that there was no guarantee I would get into a law school in the future.

They reminded me that, "I had a great job there and was making money," going on to explain that I could work my way up in the business and be very comfortable. In that one conversation, they talked me into quitting school—and my dream. I was told they were 'looking out for me' and had my best interests at heart.

For an extra bit of clarity, these men were my soon-to-be father-in-law and uncle-in-law.

On different occasions, and throughout my career with my then-husband, I flirted with the idea of pursuing a different career choice. But of course, my dreams were shot down over and over again. I listened to all the naysayers—who were always the men I was close to.

My husband was aware of my empathic abilities and the incredible ability I had to read people and pick up on energies. At the beginning of our relationship, I was spot on with my intuition.

But over the course of ten years, I was manipulated and gaslighted to believe I had no real power. He would convince me that some things were just a coincidence, or that my inner knowings were just wild thoughts running through my mind with no real validity.

Deep down, I knew I was right, but then the thought would creep in, *What if HE is right?* I didn't want to disappoint him or cause trouble, so I kept quiet about a lot of things. I would convince myself that this was where I belonged.

My family seemed happy for me, and for once, I felt like I was accepted by them. The women in my family would tell me, "Never leave that one!" So, you can imagine the shitstorm that hit when I eventually did leave. Every single one of them was against it and didn't understand why I would leave my home and the man who gave me everything (insert eye roll).

When I left, I moved a couple of hours away from him and found myself, once again, a single mom—but this time with two daughters. I left with only our clothes and personal belongings, and started afresh. I was free! Or so I thought.

I didn't realize that my work was just beginning. I had no idea of the damage that was done to me until I found myself with someone else and began the process of trying to find who I was, quickly realizing that for the first half of my life, I wasn't me. I was something someone else wanted me to be. I had taken on the masculine traits of my mental and emotional abusers. FUCK!

Not only that, but during my journey and more recently, I realized that I too have contributed to the *Witch Wound*.

As a child, I was silenced: I was not to speak my mind; I had to be quiet around my grandfather, and I had to watch carefully what I did and said so I didn't upset him.

My father and stepmother were heavy church-goers and hard-core Christians. As a result, I could not listen to the rock music I liked in their home, as they believed it was all about the devil and Satan worshiping. They would replace my tapes with Christian rock groups and pop singers (again, insert eye roll).

But when I attended Church, my intuition would kick in, and I knew something was 'off.' As a curious teenager, I had so many questions, but my parents said that was just Satan trying to steer me away from God's word (again, my eyes are rolling hard).

In late elementary school, I asked, "What is the purpose of eggs at Easter? Why is there a bunny, and what does that have to do with Jesus being resurrected?" I can't remember the exact answer I was given, but I do recall them looking at each other in confusion, and then giving me a very Christian-like answer that didn't resonate with me or satisfy my curiosity.

And then, one year at Christmas time, when I had questions about the tree's purpose and Christmas stockings, the response I received was,

"You ask a lot of questions that don't matter." That's when I realized I should just shut up and stop asking questions.

Fast forward to when my youngest daughter was around six years old. She had a glass of water and was walking outside, so I asked her what she was doing and she said, "Making moon water." I simply chuckled lightly and said, "OK." Not really understanding where this was coming from, I just let her go.

Then a few months later, she had some glasses of water sitting out on the porch and some visiting family members asked why they were there. My reply, "Payton is making moon water," was met with utter silence, then I heard, "What on earth for? What is she going to do with it? Why are you allowing her to do that? That is just weird!" In my conditioned 'people-pleasing' response, I then told Payton to hold off setting water outside and just to put it on her windowsill.

Looking back on that now, I realize what I did, and I still hold on to guilt for trying to silence her for what she believed in. She is one of the reasons the Witch inside of me is starting to wake up. She is my little Witch and Healer, and as she is going through her own struggles and finding her path, every day I set the intention that she finds her way back to making her moon water again.

I was *BROKEN* as a child, *BETRAYED* throughout my twenties, and *BURNED* throughout my entire life. The years of my forties have been a healing journey and a search to finally find me; the Witch at my core and soul level has finally emerged, and she is fierce! Living my life authentically, continuing to meditate on a regular basis, and tuning into my body is how I stay in touch with my divine feminine energy.

I now know what it is like to be accepted for who I am. Getting fully back in touch with my intuition and divine feminine energy is my goal—and

I'm almost there, although I still have some beliefs and trauma to release and work through.

Through healing, I don't think we really 'let go' of the trauma we experience. I feel we must embrace it, hold space for it, and understand that what we went through is a part of us—but it doesn't have to define us. Although I still live in fear of being seen for who I truly am and, on some level, still value what others think of me, the impact is not as strong as it was before.

Coming out on the other side of the *Witch Wound* is about finding balance, standing up for who you are, and fighting for what you believe in. If you feel you are in a place or situation that you are not comfortable being in any longer, seek support. It's OK to need to get out of that situation and find yourself again.

I promise, you are not alone, and I am here for guidance, support, to listen, and to nudge if that's what you need. I am grateful for the things I learned throughout all my experiences—the good and the ugly. I have learned that my masculine energy doesn't have to be all dominating and controlling, and feminine energy shouldn't clash with the masculine; we can achieve balance.

13

START THE CONVERSATION

Linsey Joy

Opening Pandora's Box

"**I**'ve seen aliens," I said, as nonchalantly as possible. I'd tried to sound like it was no big deal. The words had reverberated in my head for a good long minute or more before I decided to say them out loud. I didn't know how they would be received.

My parents looked up from their breakfast plates, their eyes wide with shock.

"You *have*?" my dad asked incredulously, his fork dangling in the air above his plate. He had been scrolling the news on his phone while we ate soft-boiled eggs at their kitchen counter.

I paused, unsure of their reaction. "Yeah," I answered, still trying to seem cool and calm. I felt weirdly confident and also full of nerves.

How does one start a conversation that's been brewing and stewing for almost two decades, particularly when it has to do with experiences people will call you crazy for admitting out loud?

Finally sharing this story was less like opening a can of worms and more like cracking into Pandora's box. It was metaphorically pulling a thread that threatened to unravel the relationship I had cultivated with my parents, in part by carefully guarding all the parts of me that they might not like or approve of.

And yet, I was elated by the opportunity afforded me by the topic at hand, and the potential freedom on the other side of this conversation.

There were plenty of reasons I'd kept this secret so tight to my chest, including the most obvious. Normal people don't casually discuss their paranormal experiences at the breakfast table.

But it was 2023, and Unexplained Aerial Phenomena or UFOs were making international headlines in United States Congressional hearings.

Like most of the world, my father had been reading about the testimonies given when he'd asked what I thought, unsuspecting of the bomb I would drop in response.

For weeks, as the hearings rocked the media and the world followed along feverishly, I had been contemplating jumping in and sharing *my* alien story with friends or online.

I'd hesitated to join in the conversation, however, as it would mean disclosing the other truths I'd been hiding from most of my family and friends.

There are way too many plot twists and flashbacks to present the entire story here. (It may well be its own book someday!) Still, this moment was something of a climax. Now it was out there, and there was no going back.

Demitrius & Tommy T

Yes, I'd seen aliens—two of them, benevolent and protective. A familiar male and an unknown female, both standing on my bed, awoke me in the middle of the night to prove their existence to me unequivocally.

It was 2007, and a major highlight among the many wild experiences I'd had during the time I spent with my first husband, Tommy T. Tommy had been a powerful but emotionally-conflicted psychic and energy healer, back before that was a popular thing.

He had somehow befriended the male alien, Demitrius, in secretive work I knew only bits about. I had never been privy to the details of their original meeting; I had only heard stories or experienced the after-effects of his visits.

To my shock and amazement, I could no longer deny Demitrius' existence because I had seen him with my own eyes. As of that night, I knew him, too.

I also knew, permanently and without a shadow of a doubt, that **there is more to this life than we are being told.** It was during these years with Tommy that my own awareness and dormant gifts began to surface.

My alien experience was only one event in a mountain of beautiful weirdness that changed my life and defined my personal evolution. I experienced auric healing and saw the energy in the sky, remembered past lives, heard from deceased loved ones, and more, yet I had kept it all hidden from almost everyone I knew and loved.

Tommy's passing made these unusual memories all the more treasured and sacred. After he died, I threw myself into learning everything spiritual or energetic that I could in an effort to remain connected to him and make sense of what I had lived.

However, information on these topics was much harder to find in the early 2000s, as spirituality, energy, and manifestation were not part of pop culture at that point.

The uncommonness of these events was only one reason I hid this story from loved ones. My experiences had caused me to question everything, including my religion, which was valued above all else in my family.

Plus, they had *hated* my involvement with my first husband. Tommy was full of talent and charm, with a larger-than-life personality. He was also older than me and divorced. My family's protectiveness and intense disapproval led me to feel isolated and rejected by them prior to his death.

All these years later, I was worried that sharing these strange, priceless experiences would result in feelings of rejection and anger surfacing again. I did not want to relive that experience, and I did not want to jeopardize my current relationship with my parents, which I valued greatly.

So I'd kept it all secret from everyone but a tiny handful of people. I'd protected myself and my memories, choosing carefully who I shared them with, lest they be tarnished by another's disbelief.

Until now.

My conscience had been pushing me to stop hiding and live more and more authentically. With the topic of 'non-human biologics' in the news, I was suddenly in what seemed like a universally-orchestrated moment to speak up, despite the possible messy implications.

Disclosure

There were errands to run after breakfast that summer day in August, but by dinner it was clear my parents hadn't forgotten the cliffhanger.

"You still haven't told us about the aliens!" my dad prompted eagerly. I hadn't imagined they'd let it go, but I'd relished those few hours to mentally prepare for the unplanned revelation.

When the dishes were done, I began the long, in-depth explanation of the shocking experience of waking to find the aliens on my bed. I finally spoke about the psychic gifts of my late husband, the angels and energy I'd seen, and how, sometimes, I can still hear him or others who have passed on.

There were gasps and raised eyebrows, but never once did they seem critical or disbelieving. The conversation went on late into the night. I was stunned, but relieved, to be so well-received by them, especially after such a build-up in my mind all those years.

"Well, thanks for sharing all that, honey. Maybe in the morning, I'll tell you my out-of-this world experience."

This time, *my* jaw dropped! I had been convinced that sharing my most sacred secrets with my conservative parents would result in hurt and rejection, but I was so wrong. Instead, it opened the door for reciprocal sharing as well as new levels of understanding each other. I was deeply moved. I felt accepted in a way I hadn't thought possible.

I could never have predicted this conversation would go so well. Nor will I ever promise that sharing will always turn out this way. Sometimes hard conversations hurt, yet they eventually lead to great inner strength if we lean into healing what comes up.

However, I can promise that as you practice and continue to tell your story, somewhere along the way, you'll be pleasantly surprised and relieved by the reaction you receive. Don't focus on what you have to lose. Focus on everything you could possibly gain.

Own Your Weird

The fear of speaking our truth can seem exaggerated from a logical perspective, but it's actually rooted in our survival mechanism. Biologically, belonging equals not just love and community, but safety and security on a primal level. You may think your story is too weird, too risky, or even too mundane to tell.

Let me tell you, the world needs your story now! *We are all agents of change in a pivotal moment on this planet, whether we know it or not.*

It's easy to see that crazy things are happening on Earth. If you are paying attention, it is time to help those that aren't to wake up! Whether your story involves extraterrestrials or more down-to-Earth topics in the human experience, speak so others will start to question the narratives out there.

As the world continues to shift and evolve, it is more important than ever that we speak our truths. When we share our perspectives and experiences, we open hearts and minds to new ways of being, and open eyes to hidden truths. We must bring to light that which needs to be exposed in order to heal the corruption in our systems and the things that don't make sense in our world.

This doesn't require a shouting match or protest signs. We can start with heart-led, one-on-one conversations. No one is changing anyone else's opinion by hurling insults in the comments section. No one can deny what you have lived unless you do!

If we are brave enough to tell our stories—our wildest, most heartfelt, personal stories—we will change the world.

So own your weirdness! Speak your truth! Ask questions! It's time to start the conversation! You never know who you might connect with along the way. They could be out of this world... or maybe even closer to home than you ever expected.

14

SPEAK YOUR TRUTH

Jenny Alberti

"**A**lexa, what's the definition of a Spiritual Channel?" I asked, anxiously awaiting her response. My eyes were fixed on the water flowing endlessly from the spout onto the dirty dishes in the sink. I stood, motionless, ready to discredit myself from any association with the answer Alexa was about to give.

"Someone who can establish a connection with spiritual entities to transmit messages, insights, or guidance," she replied.

Well, shit, I thought to myself with a slight chuckle and shake of my head as I turned and loaded a dish into the dishwasher.

The definition was surprisingly spot-on to an experience I'd had two weeks prior. The more I thought about what had happened then, the more memories of past experiences began to flood my mind, each with newfound relevance.

I could have never imagined the story I'm about to share would have ever been mine to tell.

I don't think I can stress that enough.

I originally intended to share that I've always struggled to set and defend healthy boundaries, out of fear that I wouldn't be liked, or respected, or I'd be seen as incapable. While the lack of healthy boundaries in my life is an excellent story to share, and is certainly a symptom of the Witch Wound, it turns out that it wasn't the story that needed to be told, at this time, in this book.

Instead, the story that did need to be told ventures many layers deeper, serving as much for my own understanding as it is for those who will be activated by reading it. It's a story of remembering, acknowledging, understanding, and healing for all the women who came before me and all who will come after me.

I've silently carried the Witch Wound for my entire life and it's prevented me from seeing or acknowledging my truth. It's kept me separated from the spiritual connection within myself—the very channel through which I can receive wisdom and guidance. This realization has started a new chapter in my life, where my mission is to acknowledge and heal this wound, embrace my true self, and share my unique magic with the world.

Quiet Curiosity

Even from my earliest memories, spirituality has always been a subtle yet constant presence in my life. Perhaps this originates from my mom's spiritual nature—from her tarot cards to the variety of mystical and spiritual books lying casually around our home as everyday objects. They sparked a curiosity that I managed from a cautious distance. She never imposed her spiritual beliefs on me, but allowed me to find my own path and to question, doubt, and explore at my own pace, as I chose.

My inquisitive nature allowed me to maintain a connection to the spiritual world, even if I kept it at arm's length for much of my life. My interest in spirits, reincarnation, and past lives was something I'd always felt compelled to hide away due to a fear of judgment and outright ridicule from others.

Regardless, my curiosity lingered, and over the past few years, has intensified as I've become less worried about what others think about my interests. In 2020, I began reading about and then researching past life regression and the Akashic records.

The idea that our souls may have lived numerous lifetimes, each with their own unique experiences, fascinated me, so I sought a hypnotherapist to guide me through a past life regression. The excitement I felt after the session was beyond words, and I couldn't believe what I had just experienced. I was even able to vividly recall a past life that revealed the root of my aversion to seafood.

The first—and only—person I rushed to tell about my past life regression session was my mom. She was the only person I felt comfortable sharing my experience with. It simply didn't feel safe. At the time, I remember wanting to tell everyone I knew that they should also do a past life regression—but I was too afraid.

This experience, I believe, truly opened me up to my eventual connection with spirituality, intuition, and guidance from my spirit guides.

Soon after my session, I found myself noticing whispers of my inner voice, and I became increasingly observant of signs that appeared in my path. The more I paid attention, the clearer and more frequent these messages became. Clues in my dreams and subtle nudges that came as I went about my day began to shape my decisions and guide me toward paths that previously, I wouldn't have considered. This is when I began to realize that I am not navigating life alone, and do have guides walking alongside me.

Despite my spiritual growth, I was unprepared for what proved to be the next phase in my spiritual journey. It started on an ordinary Friday night, and would quickly unfold into something beyond my wildest imagination...

Snap Out Of It

I could hear my heartbeat in my ears, a rhythmic thumping that seemed to echo throughout my entire body. Pressing the side button on my Apple Watch, I tapped the heart rate app and watched anxiously as the heart icon pulsed on the screen... 162.

"Holy Shit, what is wrong with me?" I whispered.

A heart rate of 162 beats per minute—that's what I usually hit after twenty minutes of intense cardio on the elliptical machine, not when I'm lounging on the couch watching TV. Panic surged through me. My skin became clammy, and a lightheaded dizziness threatened to topple my world. The edges of my vision blurred, and the room's corners faded to black.

I knew I was about to pass out.

I can't pass out, I affirmed as I shook my head rapidly.

Every nerve in my body seemed to buzz with electricity. I glanced at my watch again... 161. The walls appeared to inch closer, the space around me closing in.

Thankfully, I wasn't alone during this terrifying experience. "Tracey, something's wrong. I don't feel okay."

"How don't you feel okay?" she asked in a calm but concerned tone.

I tried to explain, but my thoughts were a jumbled mess, and the words wouldn't come out right. I showed her the heart rate displayed on my watch and said, "I'm freaking out."

Splash your face with cold water! I thought, and ran to the bathroom.

Each droplet was a shock to my body. *NO! Come on!*

My reflection in the mirror looked as panicked as I felt. *Snap out of it! You are in control.*

You. Are. In. Control.

The escalating dread was inescapable. *Oh my god, this is it. This is the day I die. I am going to die. I need to call for an ambulance. If I don't call for an ambulance, I'm going to die.*

I splashed water on my face again, and then again, but the fear wouldn't wash off.

This isn't working. What do I do, what do I do? Am I just having a panic attack or is this a real emergency? My mind raced, searching for answers, for solutions.

Just walk it off, I thought desperately. *This will snap me out of it.* Pacing back and forth through my house, I tried to focus on my breathing.

Just breathe. In through the nose, 1, 2, 3, 4, 5. Exhale. 1, 2, 3...

Now I feel nauseous. As dizziness began to set in, I sat down on the toilet and checked my watch. 165.

Oh my god, It's even higher! I need to call for help.

With my elbows on my knees and my head in my hands, I bounced back and forth between panic and attempts at lowering my heart rate.

You're probably thinking, 'Panic Attack,' and I don't blame you, I'd genuinely think the same thing if I was reading this. But what happened next was not a panic attack. Instead, it turned out to be more of an awakening; the discovery of an aspect of my being that had always been hidden.

As I sat there, a clear and unexpected 'voice' dropped into my consciousness. The overwhelming panic, nausea, and fear of impending doom entirely disappeared. Instead, I experienced a rush of concentration and heightened awareness. The instructions were clear—I needed to locate a pen and a piece of paper because what I was about to experience was something I *must* remember.

"You've Been Afraid"

Tracey called to me through the bathroom door, asking if I was ok. I'd been in there for a while, silently sitting on the toilet, consumed by my racing mind.

"Yes, I'm fine," I said calmly as I emerged from the bathroom, "And I need you to find me a pen and a piece of paper." She disappeared for a moment, then returned and handed me a pen and my Panda Bear notebook as I took a seat at the desk in my office.

If you can imagine gradually submerging yourself into the most perfect water, its temperature so balanced it feels like an extension of yourself, then you'll understand the calm, gentle, and serene sensation in my body. I remember feeling, but I do not remember thinking, as I opened my notebook and began to write.

"The guides keep guiding you…" the message began.

I remember the aching of my hand from the volume of words flowing through me and pouring onto the paper. And I remember continuing to feel my heart race in my chest, but without the panic I'd been experiencing up until that point.

When my pen finally came to a stop, a message about my life's mission stretched across two pages in my notebook. This message had a clear and powerful purpose—to guide me toward acknowledging and wholeheartedly embracing my spiritual gifts.

It was also an urgent 'call to action' for me to share this story with, and for, other women who might be on a similar journey: Women who are seeking the courage to accept and embrace their own magic, truth, and spiritual abilities.

The message was signed, "xoxoxo J," a loving reminder of the divine guidance that had just channeled through me.

This incredible experience didn't stop there, however, as my guides were not finished communicating through me. I remained in a state of pure feeling without conscious thought, with an overwhelming sense of comfort and protection that wrapped around me as I began talking to Tracey.

She quickly realized that it wasn't *me* speaking, and that my guides were now channeling their messages through me, directly to her.

They told her that my heart rate remained high, but they were actively working to calm me down. Then they proceeded to tell her to write down the following for me:

"Jenny, you've been afraid to ever mention that you have the ability to channel. You see all these people on Facebook speaking about being a channel, but you actually are."

Transmission complete, I finally lay down and felt my heart rate slowly come down as I drifted off to sleep.

Acknowledging My Witch Wound

As I write these words, I'm still integrating my experience into my life and know it will be an ongoing process as I continue to step into my magic.

I have to admit that I was a little confused and freaked out by the channeling experience at first. The following afternoon when Tracey reminded me of the messages in my notebook, my initial response was anxiety as I read the words I had no memory of writing.

The root of this anxiety was fear of the unknown, of venturing into a spiritual world that I felt underprepared and underqualified to be a part of. The revelation that a hidden part of myself was emerging, one I had concealed so deeply that I'd never even acknowledged its existence, was also unsettling and scary.

To be completely honest, I questioned if I'd made the whole thing up. I couldn't have done that though, because Tracey had witnessed it and she didn't even question the authenticity of the experience. So then I wondered whether I'd had some sort of a psychotic break.

The next day, Tracey and I attended a Friendsgiving celebration. It was no coincidence that my channeling experience occurred the day before Linsey's gathering. She'd previously shared with us her story of discovering her own psychic and channeling abilities, and I knew I was safe in sharing what had happened. With nervous anticipation of her response, I told her all about my Friday night.

She didn't blink an eye as she told me how excited she was for me to discover what all of this meant. It was such a relief to have further validation that what happened was real and not my imagination running wild. I'm so grateful to have had the opportunity to share this with Linsey so soon after it happened, because no one could have reassured me more that I wasn't having a psychotic break than she could.

Over the next several weeks, I questioned, with a mix of curiosity and concern, when, and exactly why, I had decided to bury my truth. *When did I decide it wasn't safe? Was it early in this life or was it possibly in a past life? And why did I feel so strongly that it wasn't safe to know about my wisdom?* These are answers I have yet to uncover, but I'm confident I will as I continue to peel back the layers.

As I've started the process of integrating the experience, my wound, and my truth, I've heard whispers telling me about a very important time in my life where my spiritual connection played a crucial role.

In November 2015, my mom had heart surgery to replace a leaking valve. She had a terrible reaction to the anesthesia. Once she finally regained consciousness, she wasn't coherent and was in a great deal of pain. An error in her pain medication dosage had caused her breathing to slow dangerously, pushing her to the brink of respiratory failure.

Over the course of several days, my mom teetered on the verge of a coma. Yet, despite the chaos and uncertainty, I had inexplicable clarity. Instinctively, I knew the right questions to ask, the necessary information to seek, and the actions to take, even when the hospital's answers were evasive and unsatisfactory. Thankfully, after my family and I spoke with the charge nurse, the medical team finally recognized the issue with the pain medication and were able to reverse the respiratory failure.

I've looked back repeatedly at those intense and emotional days when my mom was in the hospital and wondered how I knew what to do to help her. It's clear, now, that my Spirit Guides were there, silently guiding me through what was needed.

Ironically, when Tracey and I planned out the *Wounded Women Series*, of the three titles, this was the one I felt the least connected to. Although I wasn't aware of it at the time, I was feeling all sorts of resistance. I liked and very much resonated with the concept of women overcoming fear and speaking their truth, but I was heavily rejecting the word *witch*.

In fact, my discomfort ran so deep that I even convinced Tracey that we should change the subtitle of this book to remove the mention of the Witch Wound. I argued that if we wanted to impact the lives of as many women as possible who needed to overcome their fear and speak their truth, we didn't want to turn them away by using the word *witch*.

Looking back I can see that this was the Witch Wound at work. My rejection of the word was not just a personal discomfort; it was an internalization of centuries of trauma.

I find it all pretty incredible, really—I couldn't have made any of this up if I'd tried. My initially weak connection to this book, my resistance to the subtitle, and then my channeling experience just as I was about to start writing my chapter.

And just in case I may have missed the significance of the timing of the experience, my guides made sure their message was crystal clear. In the notebook, where Tracey had scribbled down the messages channeled through me, were unmistakable instructions:

"This is what your chapter in 'Burned' should be about."

And so it is.

When Tracey and I were conceptualizing the *Wounded Women Series*, I never anticipated the personal revelations it would bring. While we acknowledged at the time that we would be walking the path of the 'Wounded Women,' we were unaware of just how deeply each of us had been affected by these wounds and how much healing would come about by writing our chapters.

If you'd told me last year that I would be sharing my story about suppressing my ability to channel messages from my spirit guides, I would have laughed and said, "I'm not that woo," and yet, here we are.

To Embrace Is To Heal

Healing is as much about acceptance as it is about change, and I have accepted that the Witch Wound is part of my story. However, it doesn't define me or the way that I will choose to live the rest of my life. Now that I am aware of my gifts, I am committed to living authentically and allowing those gifts to shine bright.

So what does it truly mean to be committed? How can I embrace my gifts and also heal a wound that I've concealed so deeply that it's been locked away in the darkest of corners? For me, it means identifying and acknowledging how the Witch Wound has manifested in my life in subtle yet powerful ways, even though revisiting certain things is difficult for me.

I've been deeply uncomfortable exploring anything spiritual, and have written off spiritual encounters as coincidences. Speaking my mind has been something I have regularly cautioned myself against, and throughout my entire life, I've struggled to step into my full power and potential. Continuously, I have found myself on the brink of great things, only to retreat back into the shadows.

I've also been terribly disconnected from my intuition, as if an invisible barrier stood firmly between me and my inherent inner knowing. At one point a few years ago, I actively sought guidance from spiritual women online, inquiring about their methods for connecting with their intuition because I was confused about how to do it myself. Thankfully, I now have a wonderful relationship with this powerful gift.

Since my channeling experience several weeks ago, I've looked back at my life through a different perspective—through the lens of the Witch Wound. Doing so has been incredibly healing as I've recognized the Witch Wound's influence throughout my journey, and I now have more compassion for myself.

As I reviewed different times, events, and situations throughout my life, I began to understand that I had such a difficult time because of the wound living in my DNA. Protecting myself and remaining safe has been my number one priority, but now I get to reassure myself and anchor in that I am safe being exactly who I am. I am able to hold compassionate space for my past blocks, fears, and triggers, and move wholeheartedly into a life of greater purpose and fulfillment.

For those who may feel uncomfortable or unsafe embracing their unique gifts, if you're struggling to heal the Witch Wound within, please know—you're entitled to your own magic, and the world needs you to speak your truth.

15

RECLAIMING THE WITCH

Kelli Femrite

*W*ITCH.

What comes to mind when you hear this word? Scary? Evil? Devil's work? Satanist?

What vision do you get when you think of a Witch? Maybe an older woman with warts on her face, and green, sallow, sinking skin? The typical Halloween Witch with a pointy hat, broom, and dark cape?

When you think about what a Witch does in her daily life, what comes to mind? Perhaps stealing and eating children, à la the movie, *Hocus Pocus*? Throwing frog and snake parts in a cauldron to perform evil spells on humans? Manipulating people for evil, sinister reasons? Turning people into frogs and rats?

These depictions have been around for centuries. Even our entertainment industry has perpetuated these stereotypes for decades. Just look at the number of films that portray old women who live alone and are cranky as 'evil witches,' or Hollywood films like *Hocus Pocus* (which I did love as a child) that portray witches as sinister sisters working for the Devil.

This is especially true for those of us who were raised within Christian religions that have traditionally condemned Witchcraft as the 'Devil's work.' The origin of what the 'Devil' truly is, and where this concept came from, is the subject of another book, but it's a concept that Christian religions were able to bring forth to put fear in the masses.

When we start to unpack and analyze where these ideas have stemmed from in our society, it becomes very apparent that they are the result of a patriarchal society that stripped away the power of the Divine Feminine centuries ago, aided by organized Christian religions who held an agenda of becoming the 'only' way to worship God/a higher power.

Along with taking away the Divine Feminine power, it was also widely expressed that magick/magic in any and all forms was a false concept and simply 'did not exist,' in the eyes of the Catholic Church. It was not a concept that they would even recognize.

Eventually, they took most of the pagan holidays from the *Witch's Wheel of the Year* and repurposed them into religious celebrations with their own agendas, including Easter (Ostara), Christmas (Yule) and changing October 31st (modern-day Halloween) into a time of fearing the influence of spirits and evil and sinister forces.

This was previously known as Samhain, the Witch's New Year, a time of celebration and deep honoring of ancestors. Carving and putting lights in jack-o-lanterns came about as a way to ward off evil spirits on 'All Hallow's Eve.' Most modern traditions can be traced back to Pagan roots.

So if witches and magic did not exist in the eyes of the Catholic Church, how did the 'Burning Times,' come about? A time where it's estimated that at least fifty-thousand people—men, women, and children alike—were executed, accused of practicing Witchcraft?

In the thirteenth century, the Dominican Friar Thomas Aquinas published a series of written works that would eventually lead to the writing of the most widely-distributed witch-hunting handbooks in history. These works disputed the previous belief that witchcraft was not real. He argued that it was, in fact, possible for individuals to collaborate with the Devil and to obtain magical abilities that could be used for evil intents and purposes.

Aquinas was highly influenced by Aristotle, who was very much against women as sovereign individuals. He viewed women's menstrual cycles as a sign of inferiority to men.

Thomas Aquinas' works were cited over one hundred times in what is considered to be the most widely distributed witch-hunting handbook in history, the *Malleus Maleficarum,* published in 1486 by Heinrich Kramer. This is considered to be one of the most misogynistic pieces of written text in all of history. The title actually means 'The Hammer of the Female Witches.'

While whole books have been written on these subjects, I want to simply introduce the concept of how the Catholic Church, strategically for centuries, was preparing the landscape to condemn Divine Feminine healers—the midwives, herbalists, natural healers, and women and men who worked deeply with the elements of nature and Mama Gaia to help others in their communities. The people I'm referring to are the same people who would eventually be condemned for practicing witchcraft (and remember—this occurred whether they explicitly called themselves a 'witch' or not!)

Even those who were not expressly practicing magick or witchcraft were condemned, simply for being a woman, or of conspiring with women who were—by nature, according to these dogmas—inferior and not to be trusted. You could be killed simply for being a woman and menstruating. These were dangerous times.

The next time you have a preconceived notion of a Witch, know that it is patriarchal and religious programming that caused that understanding to exist in your mind.

Now, let's dive into reclaiming the Witch as a Divine Feminine force in the world, and how, by doing this work to illuminate the Divine Feminine aspect that has been previously lost, we can collectively begin to heal the old, outdated notions regarding who the 'healers' of the world are allowed to be.

This is a story of reclaiming the Divine Feminine voice; of reigniting the flame of the Goddess and everything that goes along with it—intuition, psychic abilities, becoming one with nature, and helping Mama Gaia heal from all of the continuing pain and violence that she undergoes. As Lisa Lister so eloquently states in her book, *Witch: Unleashed. Untamed. Unapologetic*,

> "It will call us ALL to take fierce responsibility in reclaiming the word 'witch' and all that it represents and symbolizes. Oh, and FYI, being a witch has nothing to do with how you dress, what crystal you use or what your witch lineage is.
>
> Instead, it's about being a woman who can recognize, navigate, claim, trust and use her Goddess-given powers of creativity and manifestation, her vision, her intuition and

foresight, her rhythms and cyclic nature and her ability to experience FULLY the dark to serve the light. And she does it to heal not only herself, but her family, her community and, ultimately, the world."

How My Personal Witch Journey Weaves into the Collective Journey

My story of diving into this path in this lifetime began back in the 1990s when I attended a Catholic grammar school in the city of Chicago

Sometime around the seventh grade in the Catholic Church, we went through a sacramental initiation. This was called 'First Confirmation' or 'Reconciliation' in which we went to church, stepped into a 'Confessional' booth, and confessed our 'sins' to a Catholic priest. After going through that particular 'Sacrament' in the seventh grade, I continued to do this mindlessly, without even thinking about its purpose or intent. I guess I was much like any twelve-year-old who is told to do something by their parents just 'because that's how it's always been done.'

But something definitely awoke in me during the summer before eighth grade, because when it came time to go back to the Confessional that year, I said no.

My mind takes me right back to the day I spoke up.

I was standing in the church as my teacher, who had been in her career at this school for thirty-plus years, approached to tell me it was my turn to go to the Confessional to 'confess my sins.'

But I had decided that when I walked into church that day, I would never 'confess my sins' to anyone ever again, especially not a priest sitting in a confessional booth. My thirteen-year-old self had her mind made up. My convictions were strong, and no-one was talking me out of them.

I still remember the look on my teacher's face when I told her my revelation—what a mix of confusion and anger! This was a teacher who had probably done the same procedure with her classes for the past thirty years, so a thirteen-year-old kid telling her 'no' wasn't something she dealt with often, maybe never. My 'no' shook something deep in her; I could see it in her body language. Her arms crossed, brows furrowed, and her disapproving stare burned through me. But I was unwavering in my convictions.

That random school morning in 1999 was a big energetic turning point for my spiritual life as I knew it. I like to cite it as the day I regained my Divine Feminine power; at the very least, it was beginning to awaken in me. That little flicker of divinity long lost by centuries of pushing toxic masculinity as the 'all powerful God and divine source' was beginning to resurface. And it felt damn good.

I stood up inside a church and went against their teachings. My soul spoke for me, telling me it had enough of being blindly obedient inside a world that wasn't meant for me. Had I done that in the 'Burning Times,' I would have been severely condemned, burned to death, drowned, stabbed, or experienced another horrific, torturous way of stopping me from claiming my inner Divine Feminine power and practicing my innate, intuitive, spiritual gifts.

It makes me reflect on why no one ever told me it was okay to step outside the box and to form my own beliefs around spirituality and divinity. Why was the only path shown to me a path that was marked by patriarchal values (women couldn't even become priests in my religion)?

I believe it was a direct result of the 'Burning Times.' Somewhere down the line, my ancestors were condemned for their beliefs. Even if they weren't publicly condemned, they hid their spiritual gifts away in fear of being condemned, and they carried that condemnation and fear within their DNA.

Until one day my parents brought me into the world, and part of my soul plan was to heal that generational trauma, specifically the Witch Wound of the past generations. It's written in my DNA to be the shining light for the previous generations who were so brutally forced to be in the darkness out of fear that they would become too powerful.

Patriarchal powers shut down any form of alternative spirituality, especially the type that reignites the Divine Feminine, so they could carry on the world with their own toxic masculine agenda and maintain power and control over the masses.

If you recall the story of creation: Eve was the one who bit the forbidden fruit. She brought the supposed 'sin' to humanity. Ever since that belief system was established, women's voices around the world have been suppressed and our divinity cast aside. Our spiritual gifts, healing abilities, and Divine Feminine power were stifled.

But that all changes now.

My story is one of many. Around the world, there are many, many people awakening to the Divine Feminine healing path, reclaiming their power, and awakening the witch within.

Connecting in with Divine Feminine Healer Roots to Regain My Voice

One way I've been able to reconnect with my Divine Feminine Witch roots is by being in community with other women who are also on their unique spiritual journeys.

I've learned that whichever way we practice our craft as Divine Feminine healers is just perfect for us. By being a part of this community, I am able to see that there are many different ways to express the Divine Feminine, but the underlying thread that weaves all of us together is that we are collectively reawakening the Divine Feminine power to the world.

We are reawakening a force that has been dormant within, that's been suppressed by centuries of patriarchal-focused societies, religions, and practices.

A big part of finding my authentic voice in this process has been to embrace that I'm an eclectic witch. By 'eclectic,' I mean that I draw inspiration from various practices, with a focus on Nature/Mama Gaia as my main source of inspiration.

I do not consider myself as subscribing to a dogma or religion; I recognize Wicca as a world religion but am not currently a part of Wicca as a religion.

The past few years of my life have been spent uncovering current life, past life, and generational trauma that has contributed to the silencing of my voice.

For years, I was too scared to admit to anyone that I identified with being a Witch. I think I suppressed it for so long that I didn't even consider it a possibility until I actually found community with fellow witches in 2022 and realized that this was indeed my truth, purpose, and reality.

Healing the Witch Wound and Speaking Out

The big turning point in my journey came in the form of a massive realization that I not only was healing generational wounds, but also past-life witch/healer wounds.

In one Reiki healing session in early 2023, I was able to tap into a past lifetime as a healer—a witch who was providing natural healing techniques for the people of her community. During that session, I released lifetimes of blocks and traumas that were associated with the Witch Wound. It was a deep feeling and 'knowing' that I had been a healer and/or witch in many, many past lifetimes. And in some of those lifetimes, I was persecuted for my practices and beliefs. Sometimes, I was fatally persecuted.

In this particular past life I had a daughter who was also persecuted for my practices and beliefs. I was holding onto a lot of guilt for her suffering and for many lifetimes, I blamed myself. The inability to share my truth and speak up was connected to this past life. I didn't feel safe to share who I truly was. I didn't feel safe to share my truth. Because when I did share my truth with others—that I was a witch and a natural healer—I was persecuted and my family suffered.

I held onto these beliefs in future lifetimes, including this one. It wasn't, at any point, safe for me to speak my truth or step into my soul path as a Divine Feminine healer.

Then came my realization that I had been seeing this belief manifesting in my work with clients. I was afraid to share the messages I was hearing, coming through in our intuitive sessions, because I didn't want them to be angry or frustrated, or to judge me and call me a fraud!

Without realizing it, I was holding back a big part of my spiritual gifts and abilities out of a deep fear of judgment and persecution. It was all beginning to make a lot of sense why I was holding myself back from sharing my truths in this lifetime.

I'm now at a point in my journey where I've released a ton of this guilt and heavy, dark energy that I was carrying around with me. I've released the hesitation to share intuitive messages with clients and loved ones because I know that these messages are deeply healing and helpful. For me, it was about acknowledging that I was holding onto trauma in my body that had been there for lifetimes upon lifetimes.

Every new lifetime we are given is a chance to heal karmic wounds of past lifetimes. I'm now beginning to explore generational witch/healer roots from my family of origin, that originated in Eastern Europe, and have been finding even deeper healing in doing so.

Meeting My Witch Ancestor in a Meditation and Amplifying My Voice Even More

During the past few months I've felt the calling to begin to explore my generational family roots, and research witch and pagan practices in the countries of my ancestors. In doing this, I've found many beautiful traditions and specific Goddesses that people in those areas would have worked with in their own spiritual practices.

One day, I felt compelled to sign up for a 'Conversation with your Spirit Guides' meditation on Zoom that was being held by an incredibly talented Dolphin Reiki Healer and Spiritual Mentor. I signed up purely to get beautiful intuitive insights and learn more information about my spirit guides, and maybe more information about my ancestors.

As I was guided into this beautiful meditation, I found myself approaching a small home in the middle of a forest setting. This small home, hidden in the forest, was wrapped up in tangles of moss and leaves. I could even smell the scene—wet leaves and fresh rain mixed with dirt and grass, and the slight sweet scent of herbs wafting through the front door.

As I approached this house, I felt full body chills as I realized this was the house of one of my ancestors in Poland, Eastern Europe. This ancestor was most definitely a natural healer and a Witch.

She was happily inside the house, working on herbal mixtures, as I walked in and greeted her. She had a book to her side, her Grimoire, and appeared so peaceful in the zone of her genius, happily practicing her craft. This is not an ancestor I know of in my lifetime now, nor someone anyone in my family has ever mentioned to me.

She told me that she had to hide away from her community; that she couldn't be seen because of what she was doing inside her home.

She explained that her herbal magick was seen as dark and evil by the rest of the community, so she preferred to hide out in the forest in the safety of her home, where no-one would see what she was doing. She also put a protection spell around her home so the villagers would not detect that she was practicing witchcraft (even though it was all positive, healing workings.)

Handing me her Grimoire, she told me that she left all her magical workings—her spells, herbs, and homeopathic remedies—for me to discover. She explained that all these things are carried with me in my blood and my DNA. She said I have access to them at any time I wish, and suggested not to think too hard about what to put into my own magical workings because I have all this information right there in my mind.

I learned that my inner magic consists of unconditional love, my healing abilities, my creativity, and my innate knowledge of how to work healing spells and assist people with massive healing on a soul level.

"You can practice in the light. You don't have to hide, like I had to hide all those years ago," she said. "You can come into the light now. Do this for your ancestor line and for your legacy. You can come to share your gifts with the world now."

I came out of this meditation crying happy tears, with a deep feeling of being embraced by an ancestor whom I never knew existed.

This is the type of transformational healing that can happen when you open your mind up to multi-dimensional healing, forgetting about time and space for a few moments while you allow yourself to be transported to different timelines in order to heal your present. I'm still uncovering new resistance within me to sharing my messages, but with each healing experience I go through, it becomes easier and easier to open myself up to speaking my truth.

I now understand that I had what is called the *Witch Wound*. I had a deep fear of speaking out about my truth of being a witch and a healer because, for generations and lifetimes, it simply wasn't safe for me to do so.

It wasn't physically safe to speak up.

As I had to wrap my mind around that concept, and as I've healed through various layers of past traumas and beliefs, I've set the stage for other women in my family to also examine their own beliefs and connections to the natural healing world.

My eight-year-old daughter will often tell people they are wrong when they say, "Witches have green faces and ugly crooked noses." She will say, "No they don't! Witches are good. They are healers."

I'm re-defining what it means to be a Witch in a world that persecuted the women (and men) who were natural healers, midwives, sages, shamans, priestesses, and witches in their communities. And I will continue to do this important work in the world—because our future generations depend on it.

It's our time to rise up and speak out; to deeply know and understand that we have the power to heal ourselves and our witch wounds. That when we do heal our witch wounds, we energetically give permission for others around us to do the same.

So I call upon you to embrace this path, to examine those dark parts of yourself that you keep hidden, and to shine a light on them with gentle self-awareness and patience.

This journey isn't easy but, for me, it's necessary if we are to rise up and reclaim the Divine Feminine force of nature in the world. That Divine Feminine force that was suppressed, hidden, persecuted, and tortured. The Divine Feminine force that was banished.

Reclaim the Witch. The Healer. The Sage. The Midwife. The Shaman. The Priestess.

Step into your healing path.

We are here walking the Earth and we will not back down. We are lifting up our voices, sharing our stories, and helping each other heal. Our mission is to reclaim the Divine Feminine and use this power to heal the Earth—and this is just the beginning.

MEET THE AUTHORS

JENNY ALBERTI

Jenny Alberti is Co-founder of the Women Writing Intentionally Collective, the CEO of Introvert She Wrote Publishing, a Content Marketing Coach, and an International Best-Selling Author. Through her multiple roles that empower women and promote self-expression, she is dedicated to helping female visionaries share their stories, earn recognition for their talents, and fulfill their dreams of becoming published authors.

Through her uniquely designed book projects and programs, Jenny's mission is to powerfully amplify the voices of all women who aspire to create an epic impact on the world. She firmly believes that embracing our true selves and our uniqueness is crucial for personal and professional fulfillment. She inspires her authors to break free from societal expectations, authentically express themselves, and fearlessly share their valuable messages with the world.

As a self-identified introvert, Jenny initially found the nature of online entrepreneurship overwhelming. However, she embraced her personality and capitalized on her innate talent for written communication, which helped her successfully navigate the noisy online landscape.

In 2021, she achieved her childhood dream of becoming a published author. Jenny is living proof that introversion, social anxiety, and fears of visibility can be transformed into inspiration, momentum, and the fuel to create lasting change. Her expertise and accomplishments as a writer and disruptor in the publishing industry have garnered international recognition, with features in *Authority Magazine* and an invitation to become a Senior Executive Contributor to *Brainz Magazine*.

Despite her strong roots in Northern California, where she resides with her loving partner and cherished fur-babies, Jenny nurtures her love for travel and adventure through seeking inspiration around the world. In her downtime, she takes great pleasure in immersing herself in the pages of captivating horror novels.

TRACEY BROWN

Tracey Brown is co-founder of the Women Writing Intentionally Collective, the CEO of Gemini Moon Press, a Certified Moonologer™ and Lunar Business Strategist. It was Tracey's love of working with the moon that led her to write her first chapter in a collaborative book project in 2021, making her an international best-selling author.

With a deep-rooted passion for empowering spiritual women and amplifying their voices, Tracey is dedicated to the sharing of Divine Feminine and Sacred Ancestral wisdom.

Under her publishing imprints, Tracey creates safe and nurturing spaces for women to speak their truth, share their wisdom, and heal the wounds of the past. She firmly believes that their narratives deserve to be heard, celebrated, and cherished, as they carry within them the essence of ancient wisdom that can guide and inspire us in the modern world and lay the foundation for collective healing. Her book projects are curated to encourage collaboration and opportunities for women to step into their power and authority.

As a respected writer and speaker, Tracey's expertise has been featured on renowned platforms such as *Thrive Global*, *Elephant Journal*, *Medium*, and various podcasts, including Yasmin Boland's *Mainly Moonology* podcast. Her insights into the intertwining of natural rhythms, ancestral knowledge, and inner wisdom have resonated with audiences worldwide.

Tracey's first publication, *Lunar Wisdom: Reconnecting with the Divine Feminine through Rituals, Spells, Magic, and the Phases of the Moon*, provides inspiration and guidance from fourteen diverse lunar women, showcasing various practices that encourage readers to create their own personalized and aligned lunar practice, and now, through the *Wounded Women Series* titles, *Betrayed*, *Broken*, and *Burned*, she hopes to inspire generations of women to step up, be seen, and join in the power of collective healing.

Although an Aussie girl at heart, Tracey currently splits her time between sunny Northern California and beautiful Northern Italy. She adores her partner, children, and fur fam. When she's not immersed in her work, you can find Tracey reading, enjoying the outdoors, exploring the world, or taking leisurely walks with her Bengal cat, Maple.

TERI KATZENBERGER

Teri Katzenberger is the CEO-Founder of the Live Well Now Academy LLC and has been a Fitness, Nutrition, and Weight Management Specialist since 2000. She is an "incredible overcomer," a divine woman who has a passion for all people from all walks of life.

As a young adult, Teri became the survivor of a traumatic domestic violent marriage, a lifetime of disabling self-image issues, a chronic health-altering eating disorder, and a chronic life-threatening alcohol and drug addiction. To save her own life, in 1991 Teri began her own personal health and wellness journey. Since then, she has dedicated herself to helping and teaching people how to live a healthy, well, fit, strong, and whole life, from the inside out.

Her dedication, passion, and life experiences make Teri the perfect choice for those who want to stop the diet "roller coaster" and embrace sustainable changes, while learning to feel great about themselves. More and more, people today want to live a full, healthy, and happy life; Teri combines her education and desire to help people look and feel great about themselves.

As a Personal Life Coach and Accountability Partner, Teri works with her clients through 1:1 Sessions and Group Coaching, both globally and in person. Her specialty lies in helping people to achieve their best life as she guides and walks alongside them throughout their journey of transformation. Teri teaches and shares hard truths to help people achieve real and lasting results.

Teri is an international best-selling author with features in publications such as *Authority Magazine*. She holds a diploma as a Fitness and Nutrition Specialist from Penn Foster University, and has a Medical Fitness Certification Specialization in Menopause Hormone Fitness, along with numerous other certifications.

Her Mission Statement is: "To educate and train people in Fitness, Nutrition and Weight Management and to enhance their lifestyle physically, emotionally, and spiritually."

RUTH FAE

Founder of Fae Blood Publications, Ruth Fae is an Intuitive Writing Coach and Editor, International Bestselling Author, Speaker, Youth Mentor, and Chief Editor at the Women Writing Intentionally Collective. A believer in the unlimited potential of co-creation, she helps silenced voices be healed and heard through the powerful, timeless, and magical process of storytelling.

Through her years as a journalist and copywriter, Ruth learned that sharing the wisdom of our experiences helps us to heal, nurture, and create true connection. In a non-judgmental space, and by working with the energy and guidance of the Lunar Cycles, she guides aspiring and established authors to align with their inner magic and sacred truth, find their voice, and release shame and doubt. Through Ruth's transformative guidance, her clients step into inspiration, confidence, and authentic expression.

A rebel at heart, she loves to challenge convention through working with publishers and authors within the world of Indie Publishing. As an avid lover of the performing arts, and with a keen interest in encouraging the voice of our younger generations, Ruth values her years of experience as a columnist, reviewer, and editor for Dance Writer Australia and Indigo magazine.

More recently, she has shared her stories about life, writing, and the power of communication in four diverse collaborative books—*Lunar Wisdom*, *Magnetic Abundance*, *Get Published*, and *Navigation Tools to Thrive in the Human Experience*. She can also be found on Medium, and loves to explore the many facets of writing, editing, parenting, transformation, and spirituality as a podcast guest.

Residing in Melbourne, Australia, Ruth Fae shares her 'Life of Love and Magic' with her partner, their blended family of seven children, and an adorably naughty puppy named Merlin.

AMANDA NORR

Amanda B Norr is a Certified Moonologer™, Healer, Intuitive, and International #1 Best-Selling Author. Her mission is to connect with and guide others to find healing and Divine connection through working with the Moon.

Amanda's card readings combine a unique blend of intuition and coaching that helps her clients unlock, integrate, and embody the divine guidance they receive. She also loves to work with herbs, oils, and crystals. Her first book, *Lunar Wisdom,* was published in 2022, and she is thrilled to be a contributing author in all three *Wounded Women Series* titles, *Betrayed, Broken,* and *Burned.*

Now a proud grandmother of two, Amanda has spent the past twenty-six years living on a dairy farm and raising two children with her husband. After selling their cows in May 2023, she is leaning into agriculture in new ways by expanding her promotions and education work. Amanda also supports her local community as a volunteer EMT and Firefighter, and loves to read, write, and crochet.

CHRISTINE FREY

Christine Frey is a Shaman and Reiki Master Teacher and Practitioner who owns Centerpoint Healing Services, in Colorado Springs, Colorado. She is a wife and mother with two adult sons and a daughter-in-law. Christine is passionate about helping people feel valued, heard, respected and not alone as she works in-person and around the world.

A survivor of 49 years of domestic violence, sexual assault, incest and human trafficking, Christine is boldly empowered to help people with her 33 years of training in trauma, Reiki, yoga and Shamanism.

She contributed to the best-selling book, *Quiet and Badass*, and has recently been accepted into the top 50 of *Who's Who In America*, having received many nominations for her role in helping erase prejudicial stigmas, helping people find their authentic voice and her volunteer work helping survivors in her community.

Linsey Joy

Linsey Joy is an Intuitive, Author, Energy Worker, and Spiritual Mentor. She helps spiritual seekers who are ready to see their challenges in a new way to shift limiting beliefs into empowered perspectives and intentions.

Since 2009, when she experienced a series of wild and sacred metaphysical events, Linsey has worked with angels, energy, and manifestation. Using her intuitive gifts, two decades of personal development training, and quantum frequencies, she helps clients tune into their own intuition and divine connection for guidance and joy.

A former Montessori teacher, she also loves sharing peace education and mindfulness with children aged three and up.

Linsey is a passionate speaker, appearing in interviews and podcasts across the globe. First published at age eight, she is an International Best-Selling Author and 2023 International Impact Award Winner for her book, *Divinity Speaks*. Linsey has contributed to the *Wounded Women Series* titles, *Betrayed*, and *Burned*.

A California native, Linsey is a devoted wife, fur-baby mama, gamer, and artist.

STEPHANIE MOYER

Stephanie Moyer is an Intuitive Empath, Eclectic Witch, and CEO, Founder and Curator of The Conjuring Moon—a Full Moon subscription box service and online Metaphysical shop.

As a contributing author to the international bestselling books, *Lunar Wisdom* and all three titles in the *Wounded Women Series*, her vision is to provide a safe, non-judgmental space for divine feminine warriors to explore, develop, and harness their own unique spiritual practices while helping them break free from societal norms. Through her own healing journey and spiritual awakening, her goal is to one day open a healing center for all women to help them on their own healing journey through meditation sessions, Kundalini Yoga, Reiki sessions, and trauma therapy.

Stephanie lives in Pennsylvania with her husband, three daughters, grandchildren, and her beloved beagle. When she is not curating boxes or participating in Spiritual and Holistic Expos, she loves to visit Salem, MA, and go to various music fests with her family.

CAROLYN PARKER

 Carolyn Parker (The Overcoming Queen) is known locally for supporting her community and her love for people. Carolyn's mission? To leave a legacy of acceptance to those stigmatised by society by promoting awareness and understanding of cultural taboos.

She discovered a passion for writing during the COVID-19 pandemic going on to publish her first book, *From A Place Called Shame* (2022), a moving memoir of love, life, and loss. Carolyn connects with readers on a heart level, exploring her struggles with openness and vulnerability, inviting them into her world. She is now excited to work with other amazing women who want to write their own stories.

Carolyn has contributed to several inspirational collaborations writing on adoption, abuse, mental health, inner child, etc. She has been featured in local and national media and proudly received the Woman Who Achieves Solopreneur Special Award 2023.

CORINNE SCHWERS

Corinne Schwers has a Master's in geography that she attained at age 50, and now is a digital companion/assistant. Her mission is to help coach women who are lost in the ever-changing digital era.

She helps her clients by creating their funnels and by giving them more visibility on social media.

Corinne was born and bred in Brussels, Belgium. She currently lives in Braine l'Alleud, in the south of Brussels, with her son. In her spare time, she enjoys reading novels, playing roleplay games, and walking.

JAMILA EKKEL

Jamila Ekkel, a former psychologist with over 12 years of clinical experience, has reinvented herself as a pioneering energy healer and creative strategist for innovative entrepreneurs.

Merging science with her newfound psychic abilities and personalised AI Art, Jamila crafts deeply resonating Soul Branding for impact-driven visionaries who are ready to change the world. These unique brands, infused with the client's Higher and Future Self, stand out vibrantly, attracting Dream Clients effortlessly.

Beyond branding, Jamila offers transformative energy healing and coaching. Her webshop features energetically infused items and unique AI Art pieces.

JENNIFER ARWEN TEMPLETON

Jennifer Arwen Templeton's life's work is to rekindle the fires of ancient wisdom and mentor women into rewriting themselves as figures central to the grand narratives of existence. With decades spent growing individuals to thrive and achieve six-figure-plus careers, she loves to pass on her secrets to success with a firm belief that training coaches creates the change our world truly needs.

Through Jenn's coaching, writers workshops, and online courses, she shares the knowledge and experience she has gained through decades and multiple certifications with The Chopra Center Of Well-being as a Reiki Master, Shaman, Mindfulness Meditation Trainer, Master Of Wisdom Davdji Academy, and Vedic Educator.

Her life, a path strewn with the duality of triumph and tragedy, is a testament to the resilience of the human spirit. With love as her compass and passion as her guide, Jenn is the 'motherless daughter' who became the Heroine of her own epic, and the healer of others. The living embodiment of her mother's legacy, Jennifer dedicates her life to offering a beacon for 'the mother's savage daughters' of the world to find their power, heal, and, in turn, heal the world.

KAITLYN SIGNORELLI

Kaitlyn Signorelli, the Confidence Creatrix, is an intuitive Confidence and Mindset Strategist. She believes that personal confidence is key to taking bold, unapologetic action and establishing the empowered boundaries that are necessary to create fulfilling, successful lives.

She offers various programs for Empath, HSP, and ADHD women, teaching them to reject society's unrealistic expectations of consistency and what is "normal" in life and entrepreneurship. Her approach focuses on embracing natural energetic cycles, embodying the birthright of personal confidence, and enhancing communication skills.

Kaitlyn holds several coaching certifications including Confidence, CBT, REBT, Emotional Intelligence, and Health Coaching from IIN. She also has a master's degree from Thunderbird School of Global Management.

She and her husband live on the East Coast of the USA with their two young children. Kaitlyn loves to garden, brew kombucha, make sourdough bread, and is always dreaming of new business ideas and countries to travel to.

KELLI FEMRITE

Kelli is an Intuitive Empowerment Mentor who empowers moms to manifest their highest soul calling and their unique version of peace, healing and success on their own terms.

Through intuitive 1:1 mentoring, spiritual hypnotherapy, energy healing, and Akashic records exploration she helps moms to dig deep and work with both the light and shadows to reveal their soul path forward.

Her personal specialty is healing personal and generational emotional wounds, the healer and witch wound, limiting beliefs, and other stagnant energy living within the body, mind, and soul so her clients can unapologetically own their personal inner power and reclaim their divine feminine nature.

Kelli also hosts the podcast Modern Witch Mama and You Tube Channel by the same name, where she shares her take on being an Intuitive Healer and Modern Witch living in the 3D world.

Kelli has one very energetic, creative and intuitive eight-year-old daughter and is married to a firefighter. They live in Illinois—just outside of Chicago—along with their two dogs, Romeo and Annie. When not writing or running her business she enjoys travelling in their family camper, being immersed in Mother Nature, flying to warm beach destinations, and reading great fiction books.

LAURA RINNANKOSKI

Laura Rinnankoski is the owner of Laura Rinnankoski International Coaching. She is an International Transformational Life and Relationship Coach, NLP Practitioner, Motivational Speaker, Bestselling Author, Astrology enthusiast, and the winner of multiple awards. Her awards include the CREA Global Award in 2022, Top 10 Most Inspiring and Transformational Coach of 2022, Women Leaders to Look Up to in 2023, Top Game Changers Across The Globe 2023, and The Most Inspiring Business Women to Follow in 2023. She coaches in English, Spanish, Finnish, and Italian.

Laura has a very international background: she was born in Helsinki, Finland, grew up in Caracas, Venezuela, studied in American international schools, attended and got a degree in Boston University, lived and worked in Miami, and presently resides in Dublin, Ireland. Her multicultural background enriches her ability to effectively connect and support people from different countries.

She has extensive experience working with advertising agencies and in marketing and sales. She worked on the advertising campaigns of The Matrix Reloaded movie and the International Space Station. She has the work ethic of a Finnish person, the fun-loving personality of a Venezuelan, the determination of an American, and the good luck and humor of the Irish.

Tara Haislip

 Tara Haislip is an Intuitive Career Coach, International Bestselling Author, and the CEO of Grounded Energy111. She helps women balance their masculine and feminine energy (regardless of gender) to help reduce burnout, increase productivity, and live their definition of work-life balance. Tara combines her clairvoyant gifts with intuitive readings and coaching to help her clients break through burnout cycles faster than traditional career coaching.

Tara enjoys writing multi-author books and speaking on podcasts and at conferences. She's been featured in publications such as Medium, GirlBoss, and Elpha. She presented at the *Power Up 2023 Concert and Conference* in Los Angeles, California on the topic, *Boss Up: How to Be a 360 Leader of Your Life*.

DISCOVER THE

WOUNDED WOMEN SERIES

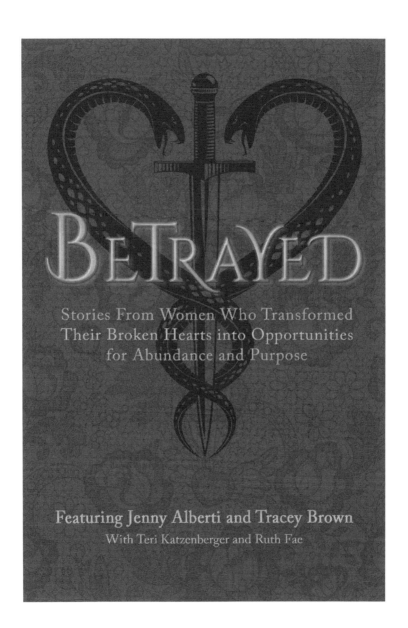

BETRAYED

Stories From Women Who Transformed
Their Broken Hearts into Opportunities
for Abundance and Purpose

Featuring Jenny Alberti and Tracey Brown
With Teri Katzenberger and Ruth Fae

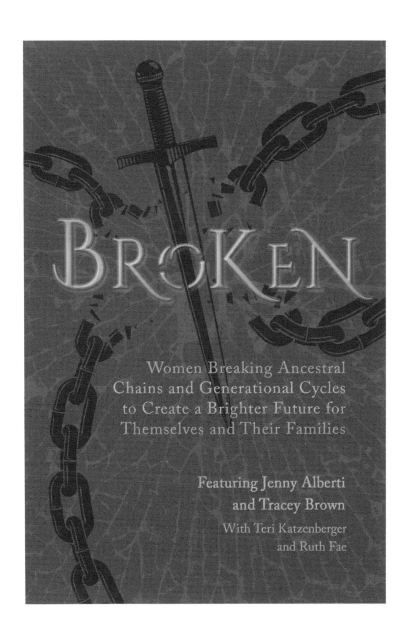

Burned

Brave and Inspiring Stories From Women Who Have Overcome Their Fears to Speak Their Truth and Share Their Wisdom

Featuring Jenny Alberti and Tracey Brown
With Teri Katzenberger and Ruth Fae

Made in the USA
Middletown, DE
14 July 2024

57301655R00102